101 *Stories of* ANSWERED PRAYERS

Stories of Healing, Nurturing, Overcoming, and Provision... All in God's Perfect Timing

Dedication

To our husbands, Ray Taylor and Don Prater

Jeannie St. John Taylor

and

Petey Prater

101 *Stories of* ANSWERED PRAYERS

Stories of Healing, Nurturing, Overcoming, and Provision...All in God's Perfect Timing

AMG Publishers

God's Word is our highest calling.

Published by AMG Publishers
6815 Shallowford Rd.
Chattanooga, Tennessee 37421

ISBN 0-89957-363-0
First printing–July 2002
Cover designed by Phillip Rodgers, AMG Publishers
Interior design and typesetting by Reider Publishing Services, San Francisco, California
Edited and Proofread by Agnes Lawless, Barbara Martin, and Jody El-Assadi

Printed in Canada
08 07 06 05 04 03 –T– 8 7 6 5 4 3 2

Contents

. . . some stories when friends pray

. . . some parenting and parent stories

. . . some stories about animals

Acknowledgments

Our deep gratitude to the following people:

- The people who shared their prayer stories with us and made this book possible.
- Barbara Martin and Agnes Lawless who edited every word of the manuscript.
- Jody El-Assadi who proofread the book and made us look professional.
- Stan Baldwin and his critique group for reading and critiquing many of the stories.
- Dan Penwell, editor and friend, who answered e-mails instantly whenever we had questions, encouraged us at every point, taught us the finer points of book crafting, and labored behind the scenes to make this book possible.
- Rebecca Kelley, Andrew Perry, and Tevin Taylor—the computer gurus.
- Ray Taylor and Don Prater who offered their emotional and financial support.
- The men and women who taught us to pray and stand in faith.
- All the women intercessors whose prayers birthed this book.

Foreword

Six weeks ago, I bought a shiny new bike. Since then I've been riding regularly, training to ride from Seattle to Portland–a ride of two hundred miles. It should take two days.

When I first started riding, five miles felt like riding from San Francisco to Boston. I came home, soaked in the bathtub, and collapsed in bed. Lately, I'm making progress.

Riding with friends has pushed my pace. Together we've learned a skill called drafting. When two riders ride together, one directly in front of the other, both riders gain. On long distances, the rear rider gets tremendous benefit.

If you struggle to keep up, you should learn to draft. The same is true for prayer. I struggle with prayer. I want to pray, but my mind wanders. Intercession feels like praying the same old requests over and over. Does God get as bored with me as I do?

For the past two and a half years, I've been drafting in prayer. Riding behind Jeannie St. John Taylor, I've learned what perseverance means. I've watched her struggle and overcome. More than anything, Jeannie pushes my pace. As I've listened to her pray and waited with her for answers, my desire to pray has grown.

Now you can grow, too. In this story collection, you'll glimpse God's pleasure in answering prayers. You'll find courage to ask again and again for your needs. You'll gain patience to wait for his answers.

Though the Bible was written nearly two thousand years ago, the story of God's work in people will continue until he comes again. He works through prayer. On these pages, you'll rejoice in his faithfulness. And you too can draft with a woman who knows prayer.

Bette Nordberg
Author: *Serenity Bay, Pacific Hope, Thin Air,* Bethany House Publishers

Introduction

In times of trouble, God's name springs almost involuntarily to the lips of Christians and non-Christians alike. Nothing seems more natural, probably because God himself placed a yearning for him in each of our hearts, whether we recognize it or not.

Every time we call out to God, every time we pray, he answers. Usually, he grants our requests, and those yes answers strengthen our faith. Sometimes the answers are very different than we expect. We don't like it when he says no or wait, but if we respond correctly to those answers, God uses them to develop godly character in us.

Most times, God answers our prayers almost immediately. I imagine him leaning forward, listening intently to our requests, and meticulously crafting perfect answers. He wraps them in gold-foil paper, ties them with wide ribbon, and sets them right where we can't possibly miss them. Then he sits back, eyes dancing, waiting with baited breath for our exclamations of joy when we stumble across them unexpectedly. After all, he's the one who said it's more fun to give than to receive (see Acts 20:35).

But often we don't see the answer-gifts, even though they are sitting out in plain view. Or we don't recognize them as God's answer. We give someone else credit for sending them, or worse, we think we accomplished them through our own efforts. So we never thank him. I wonder how that makes him feel?

This book recounts a few of the times God's children's eyes were opened and they recognized his answer-to-prayer gifts. Some stories are quite ordinary; others are miraculous. They are all true.

As you read the stories and your faith grows, thank him for his goodness. When the stories nudge your memory, bringing to mind long-forgotten gifts he hid along your path, let your gratitude pour heavenward. Thank him with your entire being. It will delight him.

Note: All these stories are true. We have used the actual names of some people who shared their stories with us. However, at the request of others, we changed their names. Each story written in first person relates an event from the life of the author whose initials appear at the end of it.

Publisher's Note: The stories in this book were written by a number of authors. At the end of each story, you will find the author's initials.

JST: Jeannie St. John Taylor

PP: Petey Prater

BM: Barbara Martin

BN: Bette Nordberg

BPF: Blanche Perry Fuhrman

1. End the Massacre

The Chattanooga Women's Clinic Inc. loomed across the street and cattycorner to the strip mall where the tiny AAA Women's Services—a crisis pregnancy center, kept an office. Unregulated and unkempt and yet lucrative, the Chattanooga Women's Clinic had stood unchallenged since 1975. No one monitored the health and safety of the girls who exited its doors empty and bleeding.

The sight of this abomination dominating a city known for its churches sickened many Christians. Nevertheless, an eerie helplessness hung over the people like smog. They endured Chattanooga's disgrace in silence . . . until 1989 when the Pro-Life Coalition of Chattanooga took a public stand.

In recognition of the sixteenth anniversary of the Roe v. Wade decision, the Coalition organized a public funeral procession to grieve the thousands of babies murdered at the clinic. They feared that only the handful that helped set up the rally would turn out on the appointed day. Instead, borrowed hearses led three hundred packed cars and a thousand people along the nine-mile route to the clinic. On the street in front of the clinic, college students held up a banner declaring the procession "In Memory of the Babies Who Died In This Place." Local florists donated flowers to lay on the line that had been painted to prevent concerned citizens from approaching the building.

The fight was engaged. In homes all over the city, believers began to pray.

A few months into the battle, at six o'clock on a Sunday morning, a handful of grieving men and women from diverse denominations—Catholic, Presbyterian, Evangelical, Charismatic—formed a circle in the parking lot of the abortion clinic. Joining hands and voices, they lifted cries to God, begging him to end abortion in Chattanooga. *Lord, change the hearts of the owners and operators of the clinic or remove them from the scene*, they prayed.

Sunday after Sunday the community of believers gathered in the parking lot to pray. And behind the scenes, the King of heaven wove events on earth.

Within six months, the fifty-three-year-old owner of the abortion business was diagnosed with pancreatic cancer. She died six months later. Her financial partner took over operation of the clinic. Shortly afterward, doctors diagnosed the partner, at age fifty-one, with another type of cancer. She, too, died within months.

Still, the abortions continued. Earlier, the two women had signed a five-year lease with the wealthy realtor who owned the building. This lease allowed the abortionist to continue slaughtering babies for profit.

Sunday morning parking-lot-prayers intensified.

On a Thursday evening in April 1993, the Pro-Life Coalition held their quarterly meeting. Patricia Lindley, the

Coalition president, had received word of a remarkable turn of events.

At the meeting, Dr. Dennis Bizzoco informed the other Board members, "The owner of the clinic building is in bankruptcy! A doctor-friend called to tell me about it. He has to sell the building, and guess who's buying it?"

Without hesitation, someone answered, "The abortionist."

"My friend learned about it because the owner of the clinic owes him $128.00," said Dr. Bizzoco. "That gives him standing in bankruptcy court. And because of that, he can take a bid in for us."

"It's true," responded attorney Richard Crotteau. "They may have wanted to keep it a secret, but a Christian realtor I know confirmed the information. It's pretty much a done deal right now. The abortionist already bid $254,000. All that's left is the paperwork. The sale will be final at 5 P.M. Monday. And we have somewhere around $1,600 in our treasury. That wouldn't even buy the sidewalk."

"Even if we could come up with the money, they'd just find another facility," someone said.

Dr. Bizzoco's next statement put the discussion in a new context. "If the Lord is giving us the opportunity to engage the enemy in battle, we dare not shrink back."

"Then the question for us becomes clear," said Pastor Bob Borger. "If we ask Him for the funds and that amount of money becomes available, we'll know that this is what the Lord wants us to do."

Murmurs of agreement spread through the group. They joined hands in prayer around the conference table. After prayer, every person in the group felt assured that they should call as many people as possible, asking for donations. They left that night needing to raise over a quarter of a million dollars by Monday—slightly more than seventy-two hours away! Everyone knew that only the Lord could accomplish such an impossible task.

God spoke to Chattanooga's community of believers, and they responded. Money poured in. One young couple contributed a check for over seven thousand dollars—money they had saved for a new car. An elderly woman unfolded a lace handkerchief filled with crumpled bills and a few coins, giving the Coalition everything she had—fourteen dollars and twenty-three cents.

Large and small, the funds came in. By noon on Monday the Coalition had $241,000 toward the purchase. Attorneys Michael Jennings and Richard Crotteau prepared the legal documents offering $264,000 for the structure. They arrived at the Federal Courthouse just fifteen minutes before the sale of the building to the abortionist would have been final. The sale was halted; a higher bid had come in. The proceedings would now be handled in a bidding war in the courtroom. On Friday morning, members of the Pro-Life Coalition arrived in court with their attorneys. The abortionist's lawyers shuffled through papers on the other side of the courtroom. Tension sizzled in the air. The judge announced that the building would be auctioned off. Court would recess temporarily, then meet again at 1 P.M. to give the abortionist time to show up in person. On the way out of the courthouse, attorneys who had been in the courtroom listening to the proceedings contributed money to the Coalition. It was clear that what was at stake was far more than just a piece of property. Patricia felt as though they were living a Peretti novel where the presence of good and evil are so clearly defined. The prayer rising from the city to God's throne room was opening the way for God to work. All they could do was watch.

Money continued to flood in to the attorney's office. By one o'clock, members of the Coalition and their attorneys carried $301,000 in pledges, cash, and bank deposit slips into the courtroom. The abortionist glowered at them from across the aisle. The bids would be in five-thousand-dollar increments. He would bid against them in person.

"My clients will deal in cash," the Coalition's attorney informed the judge. She tapped a thick stack of money and deposit slips in her palm.

The abortionist started the bidding. "$269,000."

Staring straight ahead, the Coalition attorney countered with, "$274,000."

"$279,000." The abortionist spoke deliberately, glaring at them through narrowed, malevolent eyes.

"$284,000," said the Coalition attorney.

"$289,000." The abortionist spit out the words.

"$294,000." The Coalition attorney spoke confidently, forcefully, but those with the Coalition knew it was the

Coalition's last bid. They had determined not to go beyond what the Lord had provided.

Silence.

The attorney shifted from one foot to the other. The judge looked at the abortionist expectantly. "To h— with it!" muttered the abortionist.

Nothing could be heard but the sound of breathing.

The judge banged his gavel. Bam! "Sold to the Pro-Life Coalition!"

Outside the courtroom, cameras flashed as reporters thrust microphones toward Patricia Lindley. "Wasn't that a waste of the Coalition's money?" asked one reporter. "Did you know that the appraised value of the building was only $189,000?"

"You can never put a price tag on the value of even one human life," Patricia responded.

"Where did you come up with cash to buy the clinic?" another reporter asked.

"We had absolutely unlimited resources, because everything belongs to the God of heaven and earth," Patricia answered. "We prayed and the Lord answered."

Two weeks later, on May 15th, the abortionist's lease ran out and he performed his last abortion. On May 17, 1993 the Coalition closed the clinic. After gutting and remodeling it, they reopened the building—half of it as the new home of AAA Women's Services. For many years, "Sanctity of Human Life Sunday" was observed with a prayer vigil outside the building. On that Sunday in 1994, there was a celebration in prayer as the building was dedicated to the Lord for His glory!

Because they viewed the clinic as holy ground, much as a Civil War battlefield is holy because of the lives lost there, they transformed the other side of the building into The National Memorial for the Unborn. More than 35,000 unborn babies had died in that place. It now stands as a testimony to the value of human life. It is a place where women and men from all over the nation can honor the children lost to abortion and seek the Lord's forgiveness.

Against all human logic, the abortionist never opened another facility. To this day, there is no abortion clinic in Chattanooga, Tennessee.

(JST)

"Rescue those who are unjustly sentenced to death." (Prov. 24:11 NLT)

2. Hi Mom

I didn't notice anything unusual about the top of the caps when I squeezed through the crowd to hug my daughter and her friends before her college graduation ceremony. But later, from my seat high in the stands, as strains of *Pomp and Circumstance* floated upward and the line of graduates snaked to their metal folding chairs on the gym floor, I looked down on the graduates' caps.

Scattered among the five hundred or so graduates, five sported decorated tops, as though calling for attention from someone hovering near the gym's ceiling. One quoted a phrase from a Bob Dylan song, another glittered with sequins, I couldn't make out the words on two others, but the fifth drew my attention. In easy-to-read white tape on the flat, black top, the words "Hi Mom" screamed up at me.

I couldn't see the faces of the graduates; I couldn't spot any of my daughter's friends, even though I had spent four years praying for a couple of them. I couldn't even locate my own daughter's long, thick hair. So I glanced often to the "Hi Mom" yelling up at the ceiling from halfway down the third row from the back.

I have to admit to a slight sense of irritation as the time crawled past. I'm not sure why. Maybe it was the heat. Maybe it was because my back ached from three hours in the backless bleachers. I remember thinking, oh, come on, everyone here has a mom. How come that one gets all the attention?

The speaker finished. The college president stepped forward to hand out diplomas and shake hands. I listened for the names of my daughter's friends as the rows stood one after another and marched forward. Though I couldn't make out faces, I felt a rush of pride every time I heard the name of someone I knew.

Finally, the third row from the back stood and "Hi Mom" rose. I watched the hat bob to the front then forgot about it as I again focused my attention on the names being announced. My gaze wandered to the band. Everyone looked bored.

"Dave Killian." My attention jerked back to the stage. Dave was my daughter's friend! Shortly after I met him during my daughter's freshmen year, he had shared with me how difficult life had been since junior high—when his mother died. He still missed her. I had prayed often, during the next four years, for the Lord to help Dave through college.

Which one was Dave?

I glanced to the edge of the stage just in time to see "Hi Mom" step up and bounce across. That's when I noticed the carefully formed cross, just under the word Mom. Dave was wearing the hat. The words spoke love to his mother who watched from heaven. A lump formed in my throat, tears sprang to my eyes, and I breathed one more prayer of blessing for my daughter's friend.

Dave shook the president's hand and received his diploma. But before he left the stage, he lifted it high to show his mom.

(JST)

"The helpless put their trust in you. You are the defender of orphans." (Ps. 10:14 NLT)

3. Wet Socks and Red Shoes

My first answer to prayer came in the fourth grade when my father pastored a small church in Ohio.

We were poor, but I didn't mind. I clomped up and down steps on homemade stilts, sat on the sun-warmed cement as I sanded the rust off my garage-sale bike, then practiced riding it until I could go all the way around the block without using my hands to steer once. My siblings and I climbed the grape arbor in the parsonage backyard and hung upside down eating the fruit. We explored the "underground railroad" space under our neighbor's house where sympathetic Northerners hid escaping slaves before the Civil War.

Talk about exciting! Who needed money? We lived a good life. And since Mother made all our clothes, we didn't need to buy many things—except shoes. She couldn't make shoes. And the temperature in Ohio regularly dropped below zero.

I remember the walk to school in the snow with rubber bands wrapped around my shoes to keep the soles from flopping as I walked. But often the rubber bands would wear through and break, and the soles would flop anyway. Eventually, a hole bigger than a fifty-cent piece poked clear through the bottom of my right shoe, leaving only a wet sock between my foot and the sidewalk.

I shivered for hours after I got to school.

The teacher tried to help by suggesting I dry my socks by the heat. I blushed and hung my head, wishing I could melt away. She whispered in my ear that I should ask my parents to buy me new shoes.

But, I didn't, of course, since I knew we couldn't afford them. Instead, I knelt by my bed one Saturday to tell God what I needed.

Dear Jesus, I began.

The doorbell rang.

I really need new shoes.

"Jeannie!" my mom called up the stairs. "Could you come down here, please?"

I hated to stop before I finished praying, but I obeyed and walked downstairs. June Kershner, a friend of my mom's from church, waited by the front door.

"God directed me to buy you some new shoes," she said.

"New shoes?" I suppose I sounded stunned, because June and my mom both laughed. I noticed tears in Mom's eyes as she held out my gray and red coat.

I hugged her, grabbed my coat, and skipped to June's car, barely noticing my flopping soles. How did God do that? How could he answer my prayer just as I prayed it?

June led me through three stores before we found the right shoes, red ones to match my coat, with thick soles that would never wear thin. I wore them home, and Mom had to make me take them off for bed that night.

(JST)

"Your Father knows exactly what you need even before you ask him!" (Matt. 6:8 NLT*)*

4. Etta Belle and Mack Henry

No one ever told Etta Belle she was permitted to pray. She grew up without knowing it; she still didn't know it when she married Mack Henry Perry at age eighteen. Out of desperation, she cried out to God a time or two during childbirth. But convinced she had overstepped her bounds and usurped the job of preachers, her prayers ended there.

And she needed prayer.

Few people in the Kentucky mountains lived beyond subsistence level in the early 1900s. Etta's young family was no exception. Mack Henry barely provided for her and the nine children. Worse, he studied witchcraft and enjoyed himself with the local floozies. Once during labor, Etta dragged herself out of bed to find Mack misbehaving with the midwife in another room.

Etta Belle made the best of things. She wallpapered their Kentucky shack with newspaper and scrubbed the pine floors with sand and lye soap until they glistened like snow diamonds. The garden she planted every summer provided most of their food. She canned beans, boiled sugar cane into molasses, scattered corn to fatten the frying chickens, and fed potato peelings to the hog.

Quite simply, she worked from dawn till dusk without much hope or pleasure . . . until the day she heard about the tent meeting in a nearby town. With her three oldest girls in tow, she walked six miles to the meeting, then six miles home. But in the two hours she sat on the rough bench in the back of the tent, God spoke to her. As soon as the old-time preacher gave the altar call, Etta and her girls rushed to the altar and accepted Christ as their Savior. Etta felt as though they had dug the British crown jewels from the manure in the hog pen behind their home.

Mack threw a tantrum when he found out, but Etta Belle stood firm. Nothing could persuade her to relinquish her newfound treasure.

Prayer sparkled as the delight of her life. She became a mighty woman of prayer, praying as she planted the garden while wearing her sunbonnet. She gathered the children together for evening family prayer when Mack left town for work and couldn't prevent it. She prayed for their daily needs; she pled fervently with God for the salvation of Mack and her other six children.

And God answered. Over the years, eight of her nine children came to know the Lord, though Mack stubbornly held to his sinful ways. One by one, the kids left home, and Mack and Etta grew old. Even the scattered gray hairs remaining on Mack's shiny scalp disappeared; not a single tooth poked from his smooth gums.

Alone with her life mate, Etta intensified her prayers for his salvation. When the seven girls all married pastors, and Mack complained good-naturedly that God was getting even with him for his unholy lifestyle, Etta noted the softening of his spirit. After a major stroke nearly snatched away his life and the doctor said he would never walk again, she prayed for healing. God answered so miraculously that, in his seventies, Mack was able to single-handedly build a new house with rooms for visiting children and grandchildren and an actual inside toilet. But he refused to give credit to the Lord.

He eventually changed, though, and Etta wondered why he seemed sweeter. She found out when Mack confided in a couple of his preacher sons-in-law. "God shook me over hell," Mack told them. In response to Etta's prayers, God had shown Mack the horrors of hell and assured him he was headed in that direction. The result: A terrified Mack asked the Lord to forgive his sins and come into his heart. Mack eventually became a baptized believer.

Because of Etta's faithful prayers, her husband will spend eternity in heaven. And I, her granddaughter, will see them both there.

(JST)

"Keep on praying." (1 Thess. 5:17 NLT)

"Thought is not only brightened and clarified in prayer, but thought is born in prayer. We can learn more in an hour praying . . . than from many hours in the study."

E. M. BOUNDS, *Power through Prayer*

5. The Hit Man

I tried handling the whole prayer burden alone. I didn't want to worry my parents, and we weren't supposed to tell our friends where I was hiding with my husband Ray and our year-old son—too dangerous. When I sneaked one quick call to a girlfriend, she told me she had called my house, and a strange man answered.

"He's a federal agent," I told her. "They have the house staked out in case the hit man shows up to kill us." That was all, a two-minute conversation to let her know we were alive. But I couldn't ask for prayer—she wasn't a Christian. She didn't know how to pray.

Except for my sister, no one was praying. And I'd only told my sister because I wanted her to ease my parents' fears if they called our house and I didn't answer. I wanted to handle the burden alone. But I couldn't. I desperately needed the prayer support of other Christians who would call out to God for us.

Our second night in hiding at the home of Gresham, Oregon's, chief of police, I spilled the whole story over the phone to my mother and father in Ohio. "One of the criminals Raymond was investigating decided he wanted us all dead. So he hired a hit man to kill us. But since there are three Ray Taylors in the phone book, the hit man called our house to make sure he had the right Taylor. Evidently, he heard the baby crying while we talked on the phone and decided he couldn't kill a child. Since the guy who hired him said he wouldn't pay unless the hit man killed all three of us, the hit man came into Ray's office to turn state's evidence against the guy."

"That's strange. Why would he do that?" Dad asked.

"I have no idea, but it saved our lives."

After I gave them more details, they agreed that the Lord had miraculously saved our lives so far, . . . but we were still in grave danger. As soon as we got off the phone, they activated prayer chains all over Ohio and Michigan. I could feel it.

I have no idea how many people prayed or precisely how they prayed. But I know federal authorities managed to secure a tape recording of the criminal outlining detailed plans to burn down our house and shoot us if we tried to escape. I know a rental house we owned burned to the ground during the trial while the criminal was out on bail, but no one was injured. I know the courts convicted the criminal under a law called "Conspiracy to Kill a Federal Officer."

And, even though, we did find a safe place to live, none of those prayers diminished the fear that hung around me like smog. Maybe no one prayed for my fear since there were other more-pressing concerns. But for months after the criminal was eventually incarcerated, I would glance furtively around to make sure no one had followed me home before I would turn into our own driveway. When my husband traveled, I lay awake at night, terrified of every sound.

Finally, I prayed for release from fear. *Lord, please give me a verse in the Bible I can cling to; a verse that will allay my fear.* Then I did the silly thing Christians always shake their heads over—I let the Bible fall open and pointed to a verse at random. My finger landed on 2 Corinthians 1:9, 10. "Indeed, in our hearts we felt the sentence of death. But this happened that we might not rely on ourselves but on God, who raises the dead. He has delivered us from such a deadly peril, and he will deliver us." I knew immediately it was the answer to my prayer. I haven't been afraid since.

(JST)

"I sought the LORD, and he answered me; he delivered me from all my fears." (Ps. 34:4)

"You can do more than pray after you have prayed, but you cannot do more than pray until you have prayed."

S. D. GORDON

6. Painting Away Pain

If you asked me why I paint, I'll usually shrug and say I really don't know. I really don't. I enjoy it. I'm driven to do it, and I know God has given me a gift—of sorts. I consider myself a rather mediocre artist.

Occasionally, I sell a piece from my home. But mostly my landscapes and seascapes simply hang on the walls of my living room and cram the corners of my garage and studio. I often ask God to show me if my artistic talent matters in his kingdom.

I can tell you that painting is an expensive habit. That's why I occasionally consider quitting. I hate wasting money. But every time I think about it, I remember the twelfth chapter of Romans where Paul ticks off a list of gifts and exhorts every believer to use his or her gift—no matter what it is. Though Paul doesn't mention my gift of painting—it *is* a gift. That's why I feel responsible to keep using it.

That's also why I pray every time I paint. I pray for help to do my very best. And I pray for God's Spirit to flow through me and into my work so it will bless people. I used to wonder if I was being silly when I prayed like that, but I haven't wondered since my friend, Theresa, dropped in for a visit a few weeks ago.

"We're waiting for doctors to add my husband's name to the liver transplant list," Theresa confided. "He's in terrible pain." I consoled my friend and prayed with her. After an hour, Theresa stood to go. "Do you remember that seascape you gave me about fifteen years ago?" she asked.

I didn't remember it. I've done so many paintings.

"Well, it hangs in the bedroom in front of the recliner where Roger lies when the pain gets bad. He says your painting helps ease his pain. When he looks at it, he imagines himself in the scene, and he is able to forget about his discomfort, just a little. It's the only time he feels peace."

After the door closed behind Theresa, I thanked the Lord that using my gift blessed Roger. The apostle Paul was right—no matter how insignificant my gift might be, I will continue to use it.

(JST)

"God has given each of us the ability to do certain things well. So if God has given you the ability to prophesy, speak out. . . . If your gift is that of serving others, serve them well. If you are a teacher, do a good job of teaching. If your gift is to encourage others, do it!" (Rom. 12:6–8 NLT*)*

7. Upward Bound

I recognized my elderly father's voice on the phone from Illinois. "Carol?"

"No, it's Jeannie," I told him. Blind from diabetes, he had evidently punched the wrong button on his automatic-dial phone.

"Oh, my goodness," he said, obviously disgusted with himself. "Did I do it again?"

I laughed. "Yep. But I'm glad. I like hearing your voice."

"Well, I meant to call you anyway," he said. "I remembered an answer-to-prayer story for your book."

"Really? Just a second." I reached for a notepad and my favorite glitter pen. Dad had pastored for years. He had lots of stories, "Okay. Go ahead."

"This story is about a mommy and daddy who stood over their little baby's crib and prayed for her every day."

"Um-hum." I jotted notes as he talked. "This must be a sick-baby-healed-by-God story."

"Her name was Jeannie and . . ."

My pen paused. I must have chuckled because Dad's voice sounded suddenly defensive.

"This is as much a story as any of those others you're writing," he said. "We prayed for you every day for years, and some of the times were rough. We didn't know . . ."

The years I hadn't walked with the Lord flashed before me. My parents must have suffered through that time. Since I wouldn't listen back then, they stopped offering advice, but they never stopped praying for me.

My father continued listing the ways he knew I loved the Lord. He told me how proud he was of the way I raised godly children. He had my pedestal a little too high, but I loved hearing the love and respect in his voice. I loved that he could take satisfaction in a prayer-job well done.

As I listened, I realized he was describing the same gratitude I feel for the love relationships my own children have with the Lord.

"You're right, Dad." I said. "It is a good story, because it's a universal story. Over the centuries, countless Christian parents have faithfully prayed for wayward children. I wonder how many parents will read your story while they're still praying for the Lord to save their kids? Maybe your story will give them faith to hang in there through the tough times."

"And when their children finally come to the Lord, they'll feel pretty good about the prayer job they did," he said.

"It's okay to feel proud of that, isn't it, Dad?"

"Yes. But it's not pride, it's joy."

(JST)

"Be sure to do what you should, for then you will enjoy the personal satisfaction of having done your work well." (Gal. 6:4 NLT)

"I will pour out my Spirit on your offspring, and my blessing on your descendants." (Isa. 44:3)

"Prayer does not enable us to do a greater work for God. Prayer is a greater work for God."

THOMAS CHALMERS

8. Wish List

A couple of years ago, while thinking that I hated to pray for things that might be out of God's will—selfish things—an idea popped into my head. I pulled out my special, marbled notebook and listed all my wildest dreams. Then I showed it to God.

The first was a request for my son, Tyrone, to attend graduate school in our state. Weeks earlier, he'd gotten offers for a full financial package from universities on the other side of the country. The deadline for him to decide which offer to accept was the next day. I hated to see him move so far away, but I hadn't asked God for a school close to home because I wasn't sure what Ty wanted. I didn't want to influence him unduly.

I showed the list to the Lord. *Here it is,* I prayed. *I'm only going to ask once, then I won't think about it any more. I know you can give me anything that's your will.* I wedged the notebook between two books on the shelf in my bedroom and forgot about it.

For one hour.

At the end of that hour, Ty called from college with a yes answer to the first request on my list. A university located just over an hour from our home had matched the graduate school offers from the distant schools. Ty was excited about staying close to home. That's what he had wanted all along.

God answered yes to a few of the even wilder dreams on my list, too, but they're too personal to share right now. I'll tell you about them the first time we chat in heaven.

(JST)

"Delight yourself in the LORD and he will give you the desires of your heart." (Ps. 37:4)

9. Tori's Last Chance

Tori leaned into her pre-race stretch at the district meet. "This is it—my last high school race, my last chance to go to state," she thought. "If I don't win this meet, it's over." Through all four years of high school, she had faithfully sweated through the daily track workouts, then, while the other runners went home to eat dinner, she sprinted extra intervals with her coach. She did well in races, but she had never won a district race. And only district winners went to the finals at state. *Lord, I really want to go to state,* she prayed.

In the next lane, Kate, a senior from a competing school, sprinted up the track and back. She looked tense. They had raced against each other often. Kate had never made it to state either. This was her last chance, too.

"Nervous?" Kate asked.

Tori nodded and jogged in place. "You?"

Kate nodded. "Races upset my stomach," she said.

An official in a black shirt announced, "Ladies, take your places."

"See you at the finish line," Kate said as they positioned themselves in their lanes.

"I'll be there," said Tori.

"Get set." The official pointed the gun upward.

Lord, help me do my best. Tori prayed the same prayer before every race. *Let this race bring glory to you.*

Bang! The race started.

Tori ran just behind Kate, as her coach had instructed, listening to the sound of Kate's breathing and the pounding of feet on the track. "I'll stick close to her shoulder, then kick it for the final lap."

"Perfect pace!" Coach yelled from the sidelines in the second lap.

Tori felt confident, strong. Kate pulled ahead, but it didn't matter. There'd be plenty of time to pass her in the final lap. Tori relaxed into her stride, placing one foot in front of the other in a steady rhythm. By the time Tori finished the second lap, the pack of runners had already fallen half a track behind. "No need to worry about them. I'll just glide behind Kate, then pass her when Coach gives the signal."

Near the end of the third lap, Coach signaled for Tori to move up. "Here I come, Kate." She strode out, closing the distance between them. Kate must have sensed it. She glanced back at Tori, red-faced and worried.

"You're tired, aren't you, Kate?" Tori thought.

She pumped her arms and legs, pulling up beside Kate. The two girls ran side by side now, their breathing nearly drowning out the roar of the crowd. The bell sounded as they rounded the turn into the final lap. Two more steps, and Tori surged past her, glancing sideways at Kate's face as she passed. Kate looked pale and sick—the way Tori had felt her freshman year when she collapsed at the finish line.

"She's done! I'm going to win!" The crowd thundered in triumph.

Then somehow, out of nowhere, Kate ran beside her again on the outside, passing her. Kate's breathing sounded in rasping gasps. She exhaled in grunts.

"No!" screamed Coach, "don't let her pass you! Push harder."

Tori willed her legs to move faster, but they wouldn't. As though in slow motion, she watched Kate move two, then three strides ahead of her. Then, almost at the finish line, Kate suddenly pitched forward and fell face down on the track, unconscious, her body pushed to exhaustion.

"I won!" Tori mused to herself. For a split second she exulted in her victory. Then she stopped cold, her feet inches from the finish line. "No. I won't win this way. Kate gave all she had. She deserves first place. I'll drag her over the line before I cross it."

Tori ran back and grabbed Kate's legs. Slippery with sweat, they slid from her hands and fell limply onto the track. Tori could see the pack of runners bearing down on them. She grasped Kate under the arms and pulled. As she yanked her over the line, she felt the *whoosh! whoosh! whoosh!* of three other runners crossing the finish line.

"Did I pull Kate across in time?"

Kate's eyes fluttered open, and a teammate hurried over to help her to her feet. Tori paced with her hands on her hips, getting her breathing under control. An official handed Kate the first-place marker. Tori smiled. Then sadness lumped in

Tori's throat, and she turned away, fighting tears. "I'm not sorry. I am disappointed about not going to state, but I'm not sorry."

Runners, parents, and coaches swarmed Tori, expressing amazement over her sacrificial act. They all knew she was a Christian; they knew what motivated her. She could see admiration in their eyes. *God, you did something better than sending me to state. You answered the prayer I've prayed before every race I've ever run. You let me bring glory to you.* Joy replaced her disappointment.

An official pushed through the crowd and handed the second-place marker to Tori. "Congratulations," he said. "You're going to state."

"What?" Tori asked, confused.

"The back of your foot crossed the finish line before the other runners. First-and-second-place winners compete at state," he said. "Didn't you know?"

"No, I didn't." Tori smiled again. *You always give us more than we ask for, don't you, God?*

(JST)

"Do you not know that in a race all the runners run, but only one gets the prize? Run in such a way as to get the prize." (1 Cor. 9:24, 25)

10. Wrong Roommate

An hour after my twenty-year-old daughter and her friend Nicole traipsed downstairs to chat, they wandered back upstairs and sank onto the taupe leather couch in our great room.

"Nicole needs to talk to you," Tori told me.

I closed the dishwasher and dragged a dining room chair over so I could face them. Nicole stared out the window instead of making eye contact with me. Not a good sign.

Nicole, I asked. "Did you hear from Tracy about the apartment yet?"

She pulled a fringed pillow onto her lap, wrapped her arms around it, and rested her chin on the top edge. Nicole was my daughter's best friend. I had "adopted" her three years earlier and prayed for her every day since. The most recent prayer concerns revolved around Nicole's transfer from a private college to a state university. For most of her summer vacation, she had searched unsuccessfully for a place to live—and school started next week. Did this have something to do with that?

"Just tell her," Tori said.

Nicole laughed nervously and plucked at the fringe. "It's not that big a deal." She took a deep breath and looked at me for the first time. "You know Tracy and I agreed to room together."

"I know." I wondered why she was telling me something I already knew.

"Well, Tracy was supposed to contact me as soon as she found an apartment, but she hasn't called."

"I know." Again she was giving me more old information. "I've been praying about that for you."

"I've been praying, too, but school starts in a week, and I have to find someplace to live." She glanced at Tori again, like she wanted help. Tori didn't say anything.

"Why don't you just call Tracy?" I asked.

"I didn't get Tracy's phone number because she was supposed to call me."

"She's living with her mom, isn't she?" I asked. "Just get her home number out of the college phone book. It lists home numbers."

"I tried, but her mom moved." Nicole squeezed the pillow tighter and licked her lips. Her eyes darted desperately to Tori again. She definitely had something else to tell me.

"Have you tried driving down there and looking for an apartment yourself?"

"No, but it's okay." Her words tumbled out too loud and fast. "I'm going to live with Zach and Josh. They have to have another roommate, or they can't afford their apartment."

My mouth hung open. She knew all the reasons I thought it was unwise to live with people of the opposite sex. We had talked about it before. "Nicole . . . " I began.

She interrupted. "We're just friends, and they're good Christian guys."

"I know that, and I know it is perfectly acceptable in our society. It doesn't change the fact that living with them would be wrong."

"We could have Bible studies together . . . " Nicole continued to argue her case. I listened in silence.

When she finally stopped, I said, "Nicole . . . "

Tori interrupted. "I've already tried to talk her out of it, but she thinks she doesn't have a choice."

Nicole sagged. "I don't have a choice. I don't know what else to do. I have to have a place to live. I'm paying my own way through school. I can't afford a place by myself." She sniffed and rubbed the back of her hand beneath her nose.

"Let's try praying one more time," I said. "There are three of us here, and the Bible says that where two or more are gathered together, God is there too. He's listening. I know he won't leave you with only wrong choices. He'll send along a right option."

"Thanks," Nicole said. She let go of the pillow as the three of us joined hands in prayer. As soon as the prayer ended, she left for home.

Half an hour later, our phone rang.

"I saw the answering machine blinking the second I walked in the door," Nicole said. "Tracy must have called right while we were praying! She found an apartment for us, and we can move in next week."

I swallowed past the lump in my throat. "God always comes through," I said. "He just does it on his schedule instead of ours."

(JST)

"When you are tempted, he will show you a way out so that you will not give in to it." (1 Cor. 10:13 NLT)

11. A Plain Answer to a Plane Prayer

Okay, Lord, I prayed silently. *I know I should be able to trust my daughter to you, but I can't do it unless you help me.*

I dipped a #01 round paintbrush into orange acrylic and glanced up at my daughter packing a big blue suitcase by the fireplace. "I have to admit Tori looks like an adult," I thought. "So how come I still feel like she's nine years old?"

"Tori, did you call any of the other kids from your college to find out if they're going to Oxford this semester?" I asked.

"Uh-huh." Tori unzipped a plastic compartment. "I got an e-mail yesterday. There's one girl I don't know and a guy named Dave I sort of know."

My brush feathered tiny crosshatch marks across the illustration I was painting at the dining room table. I was beginning to feel nervous about my daughter's three months abroad. That's why I had chosen to work in the house rather than my studio today. Some protective mother part of me wanted to stay close to my daughter. I suspected Tori was packing in the living room for much the same reason.

Tori had never taken an international flight before; and she'd never flown alone. She was a let-it-slide-and-it-will-all-work-out kind of person. But things didn't always work out. Always before, I had been there to rescue my daughter after poor planning caused problems. If anything went wrong in the next few months, I wouldn't be there to help.

I fought back irritation born of fear as questions whirled in my mind. "Why didn't Tori find out about Dave earlier? Maybe she could have booked the same flight. What if she missed a connecting flight? What if she couldn't figure out which bus to take from the Gatwick airport to Oxford University in the middle of the night? What if some perverted person lurked in the airport terminal hoping to take advantage of a lost young girl?"

"Young girl?" I corrected my thinking. *Lord, Tori is a woman; she is in your hands. I know you'll protect her. Help me stop worrying. Help me trust you.*

Tori bent to stuff socks into a shoe, and her long, straight hair tumbled across her face. She looked so innocent and naïve.

Silently, I prayed. I'm not worried about the domestic flight Lord, since we'll walk her to the gate and watch her board. I know the plane flies straight into O'Hare without stopping, but could you please put Dave on the flight from Chicago to London with her? Just to keep her from spacing out and missing an important detail. And Lord, she's going to need help finding her way in England. A smile curled on my lips at my next thought. And could you let me know he's on her flight so I won't worry about her getting lost?

That was pretty much an impossible prayer, and I knew it. How could Tori let me know Dave was on her flight? As soon as Tori landed at O'Hare, she'd have to dash to catch the international flight. There wouldn't be time to call home.

Three hours later, Ray and I waited in line with Tori at the United Airlines check-in. "There's Dave!" Tori whispered to us. She waved at a young man in line behind us.

Dave smiled and waved back. "Are you on this flight?"

"Yes! You, too?"

"Sure am." Dave asked to see her ticket. "Hey! It looks like we're on the same flight to England, too."

I watched the relief light Tori's face.

Wow, Lord! I'm a silly, overprotective mom, I told God. *You didn't have to give me everything I asked for. You could have expected me to simply trust you for her safety, but instead, you let me see that a friend will be with her the whole way. How like you!*

"The LORD replied, 'My Presence will go with you, and I will give you rest.' Then Moses said to him, 'If your Presence does not go with us, do not send us up from here.'" (Exod. 33:14, 15)

12. Tori's Morning Run

She almost skipped her morning run. But sunlight dappling the walls of St. Michaels lured my twenty-one-year-old exchange student, Tori, onto Oxford University's meadow paths.

Thirty minutes into her run, Tori spotted a young woman about her own age and dressed for work. She was shuffling along doubled over, crying, and holding her stomach.

Tori stopped. "Are you all right?"

Eyes filled with pain glanced sideways at Tori. "I'm fine."

"Obviously, you're not fine." Tori fell into step with her. "I'll stay with you."

"I'm okay," the girl moaned. "I have to get to work."

"What's your name?"

The only answer was a moan. Tori rested her arm across the girl's back, and the girl leaned into her. Tori could feel her body shaking. *Dear Jesus, please help her,* Tori prayed aloud. The instant the words left Tori's mouth, the girl's trembling eased. She wiped tears from her eyes and stood a little straighter, though she still held her stomach. "My name's Heather Smythe."

"Okay, Heather. Let's get you some help."

Up ahead, in front of Christ's Church College, Tori spotted a parked car with a woman in the front seat. Tori yelled, "We need help!" and the stranger left the car and hurried over.

"We'd better get her inside the office," the woman said.

Together they helped Heather into the college office where Tori sat beside her on the couch, holding her and asking questions.

"Who can we call to help you?" Tori asked.

"My mum." Heather's moaning and sobbing grew louder again. She lay her head on Tori's chest, rocking with pain.

Tori prayed silently, *Jesus, please help her*. Instantly, Heather calmed, and the sobs decreased—just as they had when Tori prayed aloud on the path.

"What's your mum's number?" the woman from the car asked.

Heather gave her the number, and the woman began to dial it. Heather crumpled against Tori with renewed sobbing and moaning. "I think I should call for an ambulance before I ring up your mum," the woman said.

Heather groaned louder. Again Tori prayed silently, and the girl calmed.

This pattern continued for twenty minutes. Every time Heather's pain and panic increased, Tori would pray silently. And, though Heather couldn't possibly know Tori was praying, she would become noticeably calmer. Finally, the ambulance arrived to take Heather to the hospital where her mother had promised to meet her.

As the ambulance drove away and Tori jogged back to her dorm, she understood that God had placed her in

Oxford's meadows for a purpose that day. And it wasn't just to help Heather. He did it to show Tori the amazing power of prayer.

(JST)

"Therefore confess your sins to each other and pray for each other so that you may be healed. The prayer of a righteous man is powerful and effective." (James 5:16)

13. Dance Stance

"I'd prefer you didn't go the Winter Formal," I told my daughter, Tori.

"Mom!" Tori sighed and rolled her eyes.

"Honey," I measured my words as I prayed silently, *Please, God, don't let me push her into rebellion and away from you.* "The atmosphere there is wrong. The temptations . . ."

"Don't worry. It's just fun," Tori said with a quick hug.

For weeks preceding the dance, I prayed for Tori to change her mind and decide not to go. Then, once I accepted the fact that Tori intended to go, I bathed the dance in fervent prayer. I prayed for Tori's spiritual and physical protection. I prayed for Tori to make wise choices. I prayed for Tori to see and accept truth.

I prayed for the teens—all Christians—that gathered at our house to fix their hair and makeup in the downstairs bathroom before the dance. And I had to admit it was fun watching the girls as they metamorphosed from barefaced, jeans-clad children to glamorous women in red lipstick and shimmering gowns.

But as soon as they left, I fell to my knees in earnest prayer. *Oh, God! Protect their minds and hearts.* I knew about the alcohol, drugs, and sexual activity that accompanied some dances. One of the girls on Tori's swim team had been suspended after she passed out drunk right in front of the principal at one dance. *Rip away the veil and make them see truth. Make them as strong as bronze walls. Help them recognize and reject evil.* After praying, I went to bed and waited for Tori's return.

When the front door opened around midnight and giggling teens traipsed into the house, I lay on my back listening for Tori.

She tiptoed in and sat briefly on the edge of my bed. "You awake, Mom" Tori whispered. "We're home."

"Uh-huh. Did you have a good time?" I squeezed her hand.

"Oh, yeah. It was great. I'll tell you all about it in the morning. We're going to have sodas and play a game for a while."

"Okay." I fell asleep, thanking the Lord for bringing my daughter safely home.

Throughout Tori's four years in high school, my concern about Tori and the dances nagged at her. But Tori always assured me that though she knew about the bad things at dances, they didn't touch her. I prayed for Tori's spiritual and physical protection every single day. Still, I continued to wonder, was she handling things correctly? Should I refuse to let Tori attend the dances? Would they hurt my daughter?

Tori graduated from high school and enrolled in a Christian college. In her senior year, a university in Europe accepted her into an honors program for a semester. I prayed for Tori to find a good church; the university located her in a flat next door to a wonderful one. Tori attended every service and grew close to the Lord and the other Christian university students in the congregation.

One Friday night about midnight, I called Tori. As soon as Tori answered the phone, I recognized the distress in her voice. "What's wrong, honey?"

"I'm heartbroken," Tori told me. "There is a university dance going on right now that several of the Christian kids from church are attending." As Tori described the depravity associated with the dance, I felt sick. "My friends view it as spiritual warfare; they go intending to witness for the Lord, but . . . "

"It's hard to witness where Satan has been invited and evil has a stronghold," I said. "Your friends are more likely to be influenced than to influence others."

"I know." Tori's voice was thick with tears. "I remember the dances from high school. They weren't nearly as bad as this dance. But still so much bad stuff happened. You'd see the disgusting things going on around you, and you'd just feel nasty."

My heart sank.

"And it didn't stop at the dance. The evil feeling would follow you home." Tori's voice broke. "This one is so much worse. Mom, would you pray for the Christians at tonight's dance?"

For the next twenty minutes, my daughter and I cried and prayed across a continent and an ocean. We prayed for Tori's friends exactly the way I had prayed for my daughter years earlier. *God help them see truth, protect them.* By the time the prayer finished and we'd said good-bye, I knew she'd made the right decision all on her own.

I've never ceased praying fervently and continually for my daughter. And prayer has released the power for God to work in Tori's life—protecting her, revealing truth, and drawing her closer to him. Because Tori was a young woman who believed strongly in prayer, she knew God would protect her friends at the dance that night.

(JST)

"Flee the evil desires of youth, and pursue righteousness, faith, love and peace, along with those who call on the Lord out of a pure heart." (2 Tim. 2:22)

14. Weird Prayer

Occasionally, I pray weird prayers. I'm talking over-the-top-ridiculous prayers that everyone knows God can't answer because what I'm asking couldn't possibly happen to anyone anywhere. Ever! I'm sure lots of people think I shouldn't pray like that.

But I did it yesterday. Just before noon, I pulled my minivan into the parking lot of the dentist's office where my twenty-one-year-old daughter, Tori, would have four wisdom teeth pulled. I switched off the ignition. She reached for the door handle, then paused and sighed.

"You nervous?" I asked.

"A little."

I assumed she was replaying the story her dad often tells about hearing a loud crunch as the dentist broke two of his wisdom teeth, then dug them out. Shudder!

"Want to pray before you go in?" I asked.

"Yes, please."

After a brief plea for God to give her courage and endurance, I assured her, "I'll pray during the procedure."

"Thanks."

Ten minutes later, as I watched her walk stiffly behind the nurse into the back of the dental office, it was all I could do to keep from rushing after her and offering to hold her hand for the next hour. But moms aren't supposed to do that for grown-up daughters, so I began to pray for protection instead.

Lord, don't let anything go wrong. Keep her safe while the doctor works on her. Don't let any complications develop.

Next I launched into prayer for courage. *Help her to endure the pain. Don't let her fear. Help her to trust you.*

Then it happened, *Help her to actually enjoy her time with the dentist,* I prayed. *Whew! How dumb was that? Everyone knows it's impossible to enjoy the dentist's office.*

I opened my novel but couldn't concentrate. Half an hour passed. I imagined Tori leaning back in the dentist's chair, looking up at him with tear-filled eyes, hearing the crunch, begging God to make the time pass quickly. *Lord, help her enjoy her time with the dentist*, I prayed again.

An hour later, I heard Tori's voice before I saw her. She chatted cheerily with the nurse who accompanied her into the waiting room, even though her mouth was stuffed with gauze. I stuck my book into my purse and hurried the length of the waiting room to meet her at the counter.

She smiled at me. "Mmgrff."

"I can't understand a word you're saying," I told her.

Tori laughed and nodded at her nurse. "She understands me."

"I do," the nurse said.

"I understood her that time," I said.

"We've never had a patient come out of oral surgery so happy," the nurse told me. "Of course, we gave her nitrous oxide—laughing gas."

"That explains it," I said. "She must still be under the influence."

"No. It's worn off by now," said the nurse.

"And you're still laughing?" I asked Tori. She giggled.

"She amazed everyone," the nurse said. "We've never seen anyone so cheerful while having teeth pulled. It was incredible."

"Oh, I enjoyed it," Tori said.

Hmmm.

(JST)

"This too, I see, is from the hand of God, for without him, who can . . . find enjoyment?" (Eccles. 2:24, 25)

15. Obeying God's Whisper

"I want to come to the hospital for your surgery on Tuesday," Kacy assured her friend over the phone. A sigh from Grace made Kacy's heart constrict. What would she do if Grace refused to let her come? Kacy had a strong feeling God wanted her at the hospital for her friend's surgery.

After a long pause, Grace responded, "I'll be asleep the whole time. I won't even know you're there. What I really need from you is prayer for protection. Strokes are listed as one of the possible side effects of this surgery, and my high blood pressure puts me at risk."

A sick feeling crept into Kacy's chest. She recognized the truth of her friend's words. Surgeries cause pain, and pain always drove up Grace's blood pressure. "I've been praying for you, Grace."

"I know, and I really appreciate it."

"But I want to do more than pray," Kacy said. "I'll be there Tuesday." Before her friend could reply, Kacy hung up the phone.

Tuesday morning at seven o'clock, Kacy found her friend already clad in a hospital gown, an IV connected to her arm. In the chair beside her bed, Ray leafed through a *Sports Illustrated*. Kacy shook her head. Men! This must be why God sent her to her friend's bedside—Grace needed moral support.

Grace smiled. "You shouldn't have come, but I'm glad you did."

Kacy hugged her. "You scared?"

"Not really," Grace said. "Patti is fasting for me, and Sue is praying, plus . . . " She clicked off the names of fifteen other women she knew were praying fervently. "I'm amazed how much prayer support God has provided for this surgery. Kind of makes you wonder why God thinks I need so much prayer, doesn't it?" She grinned to indicate she was joking, but Kacy's mind jumped to her friend's high blood pressure.

Soon, a cheerful Grace waved good-bye as they pushed her to surgery on the gurney. An hour and a half later, the doctor came out to tell Ray and Kacy the surgery had gone well. Two more hours and a hospital attendant wheeled a very different Grace into the hallway. Pale and still, she resembled a corpse.

Ray lifted the sheet covering her feet. "I don't see a toe tag," he joked. But Kacy could see worry in his eyes.

"What's wrong with her?" Kacy asked the attendant.

"She's still under," the attendant assured them. "She's fine."

"You're a liar," Grace said, groggily.

Kacy and Ray both jumped. The attendant giggled nervously. "It's the anesthetic talking. She's feeling no pain." She pushed the bed down the hall so fast Kacy had to jog to keep up. Ray strode beside the bed, his eyes fastened on his wife.

"I'm hurting," Grace said. Her face remained frozen, eyes closed; only her lips moved. "You'd better give me something for pain right now." She began to moan.

"They gave her medication for pain in the recovery room," the attendant said. "That's their job. She's fine." She passed the nurses' station.

"Liar! I'm hurting! Give me something for pain right now!" Two nurses hurried to transfer Grace to her bed. Her moaning grew louder and incessant.

When they left, Kacy's eyes met Ray's. "It's not like her to fuss like that, is it?"

"No. Something is wrong."

"If she really is in pain, it could cause a stroke. I know how pain drives up her blood pressure. I think she's in danger."

Ray nodded. Kacy waited for him to do something. When he didn't, she thrust aside the curtain and headed for the nurse's station. She didn't wait for the nurse to acknowledge her. "My friend says she's in pain."

The nurse glanced up from her paperwork. "It's the medication talking. They took care of her pain in the recovery room." She dismissed Kacy with a smile.

Reluctantly, Kacy returned to Grace's bedside where the groaning had grown worse. The sounds indicated excruciating pain. Nothing Kacy could say or do comforted her friend. Kacy paced the floor.

Ray leaned forward in his chair, his magazine unopened in his lap. He stared at his wife. "She'll probably be all right in a little while," he said.

"I'm not so sure," Kacy said. Was this why God sent her to the hospital? Was Grace in danger? Did he expect Kacy to do something to help her? She couldn't think how to pray. Gratitude for Grace's other friends swept over her. They would be praying right now.

Outside the cubicle, Kacy could hear greetings as the shift changed. "I'm going to make them listen to me," she told Ray. Once again she yanked aside the curtain, but this time a familiar face greeted her. Kacy had taught the children of the nurse behind the desk.

"Pam!" Kacy ran to hug her old friend. "You have to help me!" Quickly, Kacy explained the situation. "Please check her chart to see if she's had anything for pain."

Pam hesitated. "Well, . . . okay, though I'm sure the other nurse is right. She's a little confused from the medication." But when she pulled out Grace's chart, her face blanched. "Oh, my goodness! No one has given her anything for pain! Poor thing." Pam rushed to give her a shot of morphine.

It took several shots and four hours for nurses to finally get Grace's pain under control. Kacy understood why the Lord had provided so much prayer support for her friend.

Two days later, Grace thanked Kacy profusely. "I've never been in so much pain," she said, "not even during childbirth. I don't know if you just saved me from a lot of needless pain, or if your actions prevented a stroke . . . or something worse."

"I knew God wanted me there. Do you think he sent me in response to all the prayers offered up for you?" Kacy asked.

"I do. And I suspect he arranged for your friend to be on duty at just the right time."

"Me, too." Kacy could feel herself smiling. "But we won't know all the details until we get to heaven."

(JST)

"Therefore, as we have opportunity, let us do good to all people, especially to those who belong to the family of believers." (Gal. 6:10)

"Prayer is the slender nerve that moves the muscle of Omnipotence."

J. EDWIN HARTILL

16. Faith Versus Cancer

Breast cancer! The announcement about his former pastor's wife plummeted Kevin into depression. Gladys was only fifty-four. "She's in pretty bad shape," the Sunday school superintendent had told the church. "She's lost her hair and her strength. Doctors discontinued chemotherapy because it was too much for her. And without the chemo . . . " He sighed and shook his head. "Well, let's just say the prognosis isn't good."

A strong sense that he should drive from Ohio to Florida and pray for Gladys in her new church pressed in on Kevin over the next few days. He couldn't shake it.

"Maybe the Lord is telling you to go," his wife said at breakfast.

"I don't know if it's my imagination or God talking. I think God was telling me if I go pray for her, he'll heal her. I feel compelled to do it. But what if I go down there and pray in front of a bunch of people and she dies anyway? I'd hate looking like a fool."

"You don't want to go unless the idea came from God. But if God is telling you to go . . ." She placed a plate of scrambled eggs and sausage in front of him. "When would you have the time? You have to work."

"I have that all figured out. If I left here Saturday morning and drove all day and most of the night, I'd get to Florida in time to take a nap before church Sunday morning." He stabbed a bite of sausage and shoved it into his mouth, watching for her reaction to his words.

"How would you pay for the gas? A trip like that costs money."

"That I haven't figured out." Only the sound of forks clicking on stoneware broke the silence for a while.

"Honey," Kevin said.

His wife bit off a piece of toast. "Hmm?"

"You know I've been thinking about selling my trailer. What if we put out a fleece? Let's ask God to help us sell the trailer if this is his idea and not just my imagination. Then if it sells, we'll know he's prompting me. Plus, that'll also pay for the trip."

"Okay."

They prayed together before Kevin left for work. They didn't advertise the trailer or tell anyone it was for sale. All that week, he waited to see what would happen. Nothing happened . . . until Friday evening.

A friend from church pulled into the driveway and pointed at the trailer. "Kev, you want to sell that thing?"

"Sure do."

"How much?"

Kevin had already calculated the cost of the trip. He named that figure, and the two friends shook hands on the deal. Saturday morning, Kevin left for Florida.

Sunday morning, when Pastor Clare and Gladys walked up to the church, Kevin waited for them on the steps. He was shocked at how ill Gladys looked.

"My goodness, Kevin!" Pastor Clare exclaimed. "What in the world are you doing here?"

"I came to pray for Gladys."

Pastor Clare glanced at his wife. "We don't customarily have special prayer services on a Sunday morning. Could you wait for the evening service?"

Kevin agreed. He declined the pastor's lunch invitation, sleeping on the couch in the church office instead. That evening, he waited in a back pew until the singing ended and the congregation had gathered in the front to pray for Gladys. Then Kevin walked to the front. Kneeling on one knee behind her, he placed his hand on top of her head. He felt her wig shift under the weight of his hand. He didn't care if he looked foolish to Gladys and Clare, he didn't care if he looked foolish to the congregation. He simply desired to please God.

God, Kevin prayed, *you said if I'd come down here and pray for Gladys, you'd heal her. Well, I did. Thank you.*

That was it.

Rising to his feet, Kevin turned, walked out of the church, and drove home in time for work on Monday morning. He had obeyed God, and it felt great.

Was Gladys healed? Despite the fact that she lost five dear friends to breast cancer within five years of her own diagnosis and surgery, today Gladys is alive and well at age eighty. She has been cancer-free for over twenty years. Praise the Lord for his healing power . . . and Kevin's faith!

(JST)

"In those days Hezekiah became ill and was at the point of death. He prayed to the L*ORD, who answered him and gave him a miraculous sign."* (2 Chron. 32:24)

17. Take That Job and Quit It

Every Monday for nearly a year, I drove to Judy's office at noon. She would skip lunch and hurry downstairs. Then we would sit in my blue minivan in a parking lot overlooking wetlands just a block from her office and pray until her lunchtime ended. We had no other time to meet for prayer because her husband insisted she work outside the home.

During that whole year, we begged the Lord to release her to stay home and care for her house and husband. Her heart burned for time to minister to the people that came across her path. We prayed for it every Monday.

Nothing happened. Then one day as I was praying alone in my living room, a sudden surge of faith swept over me—I don't know how else to describe it. I leapt to my feet, pacing the room. I had to hold myself back to keep from shouting the prayer: *Lord, make Mike tell Judy she can quit work. Let it be completely his idea. Then don't let him change his mind or regret it.* I lifted my arms to heaven. I knew. I knew Mike would tell her to quit work.

Three days later, Judy called. Mike had told her to quit work. We rejoiced over the phone, but I wasn't surprised.

That has happened to me before. A surge of faith yanks me to my feet, and the prayer is answered quickly. The thing I don't understand is: Does God pour out needed faith when he's ready to act? Or does our strong faith get God's attention? I don't know, but today I plan to pray, *Lord, increase my faith!*

(JST)

"The apostles said to the Lord, 'Increase our faith!' He replied, 'If you have faith as small as a mustard seed, you can say to this mulberry tree, "Be uprooted and planted in the sea," and it will obey you.'" (Luke 17: 5, 6)

"If I should neglect prayer but a single day,
I should lose a great deal of the fire of faith."

MARTIN LUTHER

18. Painted into a Corner by Prayer

Five days after Eleanor wrote her picture book about heaven, she received a verbal commitment from a small publishing house that they would publish it. The next day, she started sketching the illustrations. Six months later, the publisher sent her a contract to sign.

"I don't want to sign unless I can illustrate it," she told the editor.

He knew her artwork. "You've got the job if you want it," he promised.

Though he didn't include illustrating in the contract, she signed the contract anyway. She knew him. He would stick to his word. She didn't need it in writing.

She had hundreds of hours invested in the paintings and about two thirds of them finished when the Jones family reunion rolled around. She packed them into the bottom of her luggage and hauled them off to Michigan. Her aunts, uncles, and cousins cried when she read the story to them. They stared amazed at the pictures, reaching out to trace details with their fingers. They loved the story. They loved the pictures. Eleanor loved the story. Eleanor loved the pictures.

So why did she suddenly begin to see them differently when she arrived home from the trip? In one painting, the girl's eyes didn't look quite right, too round. In another both kids looked—she didn't know—stiff. Vague dissatisfaction plagued her whenever she painted. She started thinking she shouldn't be wasting her time doing artwork because it kept her from writing, and she needed to write.

So when two artist friends came to visit, she dragged the illustrations out to show them. Their reactions confirmed what she'd been thinking. The paintings were okay but not the excellent quality she wanted for her book. She called the publisher.

"John, I'm not sure I want to illustrate the book. If you have another artist, go ahead and assign the manuscript to her."

"This is incredible." He chuckled, and she could almost hear him shaking his head over the phone. "Last week I handed an artist a stack of manuscripts and asked her which one she wanted to illustrate. I didn't realize your story was in the pile until she chose it."

"Is she good?" Eleanor asked.

"She's fabulous. But I told her she couldn't have that one because I had promised the author she could do it herself. The illustrator begged for it. I said no. She kept insisting she had to illustrate yours. Finally, I told her the only way she would get it was to pray."

"That was last week?" Eleanor asked. She tried to remember when she started disliking her drawings. It was about that time.

"Uh-huh, last week. Then two days ago she called to say she had several people at her church praying for the author to change her mind."

"And I did! You're right, that is incredible. Prayer is powerful!"

They hung up, and the publisher commissioned the praying artist to be the illustrator for Eleanor's book.

(JST)

"Many are the plans in a man's heart, but it is the LORD's purpose that prevails." (Prov. 19:21)

19. Jump-Starting a Dead Friendship

It was a misunderstanding. Patti saw the problem from one perspective and Bonnie saw it from another. Bonnie, angry and hurt, pulled away and allowed the friendship to disintegrate.

Patti prayed, *Lord, I've fasted and sought you. I don't feel there was any error on my part. Help me know what to do. We're in the same church, so help us settle this and find unity again.*

"Go to her and share your perspective one more time," was all Patti sensed as she prayed.

All right, Lord, I'll go if you'll help me, Patti promised.

So they met, talked, and prayed. Patti even included Bonnie's husband in the meeting, hoping his male viewpoint would shed light on their problem. But nothing was resolved. A short time later, Bonnie and her husband left the church and found a new place to worship.

Heavyhearted, Patti prayed daily for Bonnie. *Oh Lord, I feel terrible. Is it my fault they left our church fellowship? Show me if I'm in error,* she pleaded. But God seemed to have nothing more to say. *Lord, I've done all I know to do. I leave it in your hands.* Gradually, Patti forgot about the situation.

A year later, Patti arrived at church for women's Bible study. And who should be there but Bonnie! "What a surprise to see Bonnie back," Patti mused. "I need to make her feel welcome."

The meeting ended, and the women hurried off to other responsibilities. Only Patti, Bonnie, and Edna, an elderly friend, remained. "I feel so weak and faint lately," Edna said. "Will you ladies pray for me?"

As the two women prayed for their friend, Patti was surprised. The tension between them seemed to be gone. "Well, maybe everything is settled after all," she thought. Patti prayed silently. *Lord, I'd like to know for sure that Bonnie has forgiven me. Could you have Bonnie reach out to me in a special way if everything really is okay? Lord, it would help so much to know for sure.*

When prayer for Edna ended, Patti walked to her car only to discover it wouldn't start. "Why won't the car start? I've never had problems with the battery before."

Walking into the church office, Patti approached the secretary, "My battery seems to be dead.

Could someone help me start my car with their jumper cables?"

"I've got some cables. I'll help you. It'll only take a minute to pull my car up next to yours," came a voice from the corner of the room. Patti turned to see Bonnie smiling at her.

"Thanks, Bonnie," Patti grinned back. *And thanks to you, too, Lord.* From then on, the friendship and the battery purred along without a glitch.

(PP)

"If you forgive anyone, I also forgive him. And what I have forgiven—if there was anything to forgive—I have forgiven in the sight of Christ for your sake, in order that Satan might not outwit us." (2 Cor. 2:10, 11)

20. Sharing Suffer-ring

Seated at her office desk, Sandy watched the whole scene unfold. Janice stood before her mother's desk. Her shoulders drooped; her face flushed. She couldn't look her mom in the eye. Sandy's heart went out to this young woman; she knew from experience what would happen next.

"Mom, I lost the ring you gave me for high school graduation. I'm so sorry. I was at the mall and . . . " Janice's voice trailed off.

Margaret, Janice's mother, was the office supervisor. Her attitude was constantly negative, endlessly criticizing everyone's work. It wasn't difficult to know what Margaret's reaction would be to the news of the lost ring. Margaret exploded. "You get over to the mall right now and find that ring, young lady, I spent a lot of money for it!"

Sandy winced. "Poor kid's got enough problems already. Now this," she thought. Janice had been injured as a child and still limped badly. Sandy knew how tough life could be for kids with disabilities. Her heart ached for Janice.

The teen's face crumpled under her mother's public tongue-lashing. "I will, Mom. I'll go back right now. Maybe I can find it." Her voice quivered as she tried to appease her mother. Then she was gone.

Closing her eyes at her desk, Sandy silently prayed. *Oh Lord, help her find that ring so Margaret won't be angry with her. Thank you, Father.*

Twenty minutes later, Sandy heard the phone ring at Margaret's desk. Margaret growled into the mouthpiece, "Well, it's a good thing." Then she hung up the receiver. Turning to Sandy, she said, "Janice found the ring. It was laying on the mall floor outside the door of the last store where she shopped."

Gratitude rose spontaneously in Sandy's heart. *Thank you, thank you, thank you, Lord!*

(PP)

"Then you will call, and the LORD will answer; you will cry for help, and he will say: Here am I." (Isa. 58:9)

21. Emmanuel Earrings

News of a suspicious spot on her mammogram would have been a blow to Cathy under the best of circumstances. But today, after weeks of watching her friend Gail suffer the ill effects of breast cancer, the news pushed Cathy over the edge.

She trembled so violently she could barely unlock the car door and drive home from the clinic. "I'll go bald," she thought. A picture of her young daughter flashed before her, and tears spilled from her eyes. "Will I see my daughter grow up and get married?" Fear coiled in her stomach like a nest of rattlers.

Pulling up the driveway, she stumbled into the house and through her bedroom door. She flung herself across the bed sobbing, *Help me, God. Give me peace. I want your will, but I'm terrified. I can't get through this unless you give me your peace.*

Twenty minutes later, God powerfully answered her prayer. A blanket of peace enfolded her as though she had crossed through a threshold. The peace came from God's presence, and Cathy knew, beyond any doubt, he would be with her through whatever happened.

A few days later, a second mammogram proved normal. But the experience helped Cathy understand the fear threatening to overpower Gail. For the first time, she knew how to minister to her friend and assure her that God was with her.

For Christmas that year, the two friends pierced the top of their left ears and inserted small gold hoops. They call the hoops their Emmanuel—God with us—earrings. They wear them to this day as a reminder that God not only stayed with Gail through her cancer treatments, but he will stay with both of them, always . . . whether he chooses to cure Gail's cancer or not.

(JST)

"So do not fear, for I am with you; do not be dismayed, for I am your God. I will strengthen you and help you; I will uphold you with my righteous right hand." (Isa. 41:10)

"When you praise God in the midst of a trial, you cooperate with his plan to remove the scum; when you complain, you resist his plan and stir the impurities right back into your character."

RUTH MYERS, *31 Days of Praise*

22. Can-Do Faye

Faye Schleutker is a *can-do* kind of gal. When the pastor of her church in Gold Shores, Alabama, asked if she could reorganize the archives of the church library, she immediately answered, "Sure. I can do that." She responded the same way when he wanted her to fold bulletins and sew patchwork lap robes for a nearby nursing home.

So of course, when Ash Wednesday rolled around and the church needed someone to plan the traditional luncheon for the women "snowbirds," retirees who winter in Gold Shores, Faye volunteered and recruited her Bible study to help. They would serve egg-salad sandwiches and cake to the seventy-five women while their husbands enjoyed a sunny afternoon on the golf course. No problem.

Except . . .

Rain swept the golf course that day. It came down in torrents and offered no sign of relenting. Dedicated golfers abandoned the soggy grass and surged into the church for a free lunch. They must have invited their nonchurched friends, too. Instead of the anticipated seventy-five eat-like-a-bird ladies, there now stood almost two hundred ravenous snowbirds waiting in the egg-salad line. Obviously, there wasn't enough food.

What to do? Faye and her Bible study huddled together in panic. Faye suggested they pray. And during the prayer, an idea came to Millie Rice. “Let’s give each of them half a sandwich instead of a whole one and a small piece of cake,” she said. “Then if there are leftovers, they can come for seconds.” The women all agreed.

The serving line felt like a prayer meeting for Faye that day as she focused on the Lord, trusting him to stretch the food. She felt his strong presence the whole time. And, strangely, the pile of sandwiches never seemed to go down—though everyone had plenty to eat. After the luncheon, the Bible study ladies encircled the food trays, staring at it in awe.

“Do you think Jesus actually multiplied the food like he did when he fed the five thousand?” Millie asked in a hushed voice.

“I don’t know . . .” Faye had wondered the same thing. “Maybe he just made everyone fill up on half a sandwich and a small piece of cake. Whatever happened, I know God did it. I felt him here with us.”

“Me, too!” said Millie.

(JST)

“They all ate and were satisfied, and the disciples picked up twelve basketfuls of broken pieces that were left over.” (Luke 9:17)

23. Chronic Pain

I awakened in pain—again—my shoulder throbbing with the chronic ache that had plagued me for eleven years. "Oh, Lord, I need my sleep," I moaned, glancing at the time on my digital alarm—1:13 AM. I'd been awake at least four times since I went to bed at ten o'clock. I'd be too tired to work tomorrow.

I rolled onto my side, fighting the loneliness that always accompanied the pain. Would the night never end? *Please help me sleep,* I prayed.

Kneading my shoulder and arm, I traipsed to the bathroom to find an aspirin, but I didn't have much hope it would work. It rarely did. But tonight, for some reason, the small pill worked wonders. The moment my head touched the pillow, I fell into a deep sleep. When the alarm rang at 7 AM, I awakened refreshed, unable to remember any pain after I took the aspirin.

"Wow! I wonder how aspirin suddenly turned into a miracle drug," I said to the mirror the next morning. My day, also, went well; the good night's sleep energized me.

In the late afternoon, my phone rang. "I talked to Marilyn this morning," Barb said.

"Oh? How is she?"

"She said that last night she woke up in the middle of the night and felt the need to pray for you. So she prayed for a long time, but she has no idea why."

"Oh, my goodness. I know why." I then explained about my pain from the night before. "I thought it was strange for the aspirin to help me so much when it never had before."

"It sounds like it's more than the aspirin."

"You're right. I'm sure Marilyn's prayer allowed me to sleep."

My chronic pain didn't feel quite so lonely from then on. I knew God understood what I was going through. And I knew he'd lay it on someone's heart to pray for me when I desperately needed it.

(JST)

"You know when I sit and when I rise; you perceive my thoughts from afar. You discern my going out and my lying down; you are familiar with all my ways." (Ps. 139:2, 3)

24. Grounded

This is Roman's story, but he knows nothing about it, and I doubt he ever will. It started one Saturday in September when his mother, Shirley, confided in me about a trip her twenty-eight-year-old son had planned with an older woman. Though the woman was a mother and grandmother, Roman found her attractive and planned to spend the following weekend with her in Los Angeles. He had already purchased the plane tickets.

I felt sick.

I prayed for him on and off all weekend. Then Monday evening, my fingers flew over the keyboard, typing a prayer onto an e-mail to send to Roman's mother. *Lord, in the name of Jesus, I plead for protection for Roman,* I typed. *Replace his noodle of a backbone with a steel rod. Soften his hard, rebellious heart. Keep him isolated from the evil influence of this woman until he is strong enough to resist temptation.*

I knew Shirley would pray with me as she read the e-mail, so I continued, *Lord, don't let Satan and his demons win out in this situation. I plead with you to intervene. Don't allow Roman to fly to Los Angeles this weekend.*

Part of me prayed in faith and strongly believed Roman wouldn't fly to Los Angeles; another part of me knew the prayer couldn't possibly be answered. The airline ticket was already paid for, the hotel room reserved. What could cause Roman to change his mind?

The next morning, September 11, 2001, all airplanes in the United States were grounded for the first time in history. Roman did not go to Los Angeles.

Do I think my prayer had anything to do with causing a national tragedy? Absolutely not! But our amazing Lord is able to pull good out of anything.

(JST)

"And we know that in all things God works for the good of those who love him, who have been called according to his purpose." (Rom. 8:28)

25. Noise in the Waiting Room

I opened my mouth to protest when Cherie prayed a prayer that couldn't be answered: *Lord, let friends flock around Jeannie's mom during her dad's bypass surgery. Let them flow in from every direction and fill the waiting room.*

I started to say, "Don't bother praying that prayer. My parents were elderly when they moved to Bloomington. They never made any close friends there. They rarely get to church. My brother, Karl, has to work during the surgery. I live three thousand miles away. My sister, Jodi, will stay with my mom, but there's no one else."

But instead, I just kept my eyes closed and said nothing.

The next afternoon, I called the cardiac waiting room in Bloomington, Illinois, and asked to speak to my mother.

"What? I can't hear you. It's too noisy in here," said the lady who answered the phone.

"What in the world could cause noise in a hospital waiting room?" ran through my mind. I enunciated my mother's name into the phone. This time the lady understood, and in a few seconds my mother answered.

"Your father had five bypasses, and he's doing better than expected," my mother said. She seemed to be shouting over a tangle of voices in the background. And she sounded rather chipper, considering the dire situation.

"Jodi and Rus are here," my mother continued, "and Rus's brother Ron drove down from Chicago, and Karl and Judy came over from Galesburg, and Chelise and Jerry came from Kankakee. Nate and Tonia took off work and brought Shaelah. And Adam is here. Oh, and my friend Carolyn," she paused before adding, "and our pastor."

Finally, I understood how a cardiac waiting room could sound so noisy. All the people I thought couldn't come for my dad's surgery had come. And people I would never have thought of showed up, too. God had answered Cherie's impossible prayer.

(JST)

"Each of you should look not only to your own interests, but also to the interests of others." (Phil. 2:4)

26. Rescued

It is my belief that the Lord directs us how to pray—if we just listen.

I'm not a particularly good listener, but fortunately, the Lord is willing to shout at me when he has to. And though I didn't realize it at the time, that's what he was doing the year my shy youngest son attended kindergarten.

For three weeks, I felt the urgent need to pray for protection for my children. I always pray daily for their safety, of course, but this was different. When I say urgent, I mean urgent. So I prayed nonstop for three weeks.

But strangely, the morning it happened, I didn't feel any sense of danger. I stayed in the car with my engine running while I saw Tevin enter the school building. I watched through the large windows until I saw his head join the group of twenty heads bobbing around Mrs. Byrne's waist. Then I drove the circuitous route back to my house and pulled in at the school next door where I would spend the morning volunteering in another classroom. Interestingly, I specifically remember thinking how good it made me feel to see him safely with Mrs. Byrne.

But Tevin wasn't safe. I had made a terrible mistake. The children surrounding Mrs. Byrne were not from Tevin's classroom. For some reason, the principal had cancelled morning kindergarten that day, and somehow, I hadn't seen the notice. The youngsters milling around Mrs. Byrne were from the afternoon class. Tevin didn't know any of them.

As soon as Tevin realized something was wrong, he slipped out of the building, terrified. He was alone in the big city.

After I finished my two hours of volunteering, I stopped at the store for a few things, and then hurried home to put the groceries away before I returned to pick up Tevin. I could hear the phone ringing as I drove up. I rushed to unlock the door and answer it.

"Hello?"

The voice of Debbie Higgins, a single mother of five who drove around in a rusted Volkswagen van and baby-sat children to earn a living, greeted me. "Hi, it's Debbie."

"Debbie!" Sweet lady, I thought.

"I have Tevin at home with me."

"What? How . . . " I couldn't think. "No. Tevin's at school."

"They cancelled morning kindergarten," she told me. "When I dropped off Eddie, I spotted Tevin hiding in the bushes, crying. So I brought him here. He's been with me all morning."

My head and heart whirled together, dancing through confused, terrified, happy emotions all mixed together. "Oh, Debbie. You probably saved his life."

"Very possibly," she agreed.

"I think the Lord sent you."

"I'm sure of it."

After that, the urgent prodding to pray for protection left, and I returned to my customary daily prayers. I often wonder what would have happened to my little boy if God hadn't urged me to pray, then answered that prayer by sending Debbie along at just the right time. Every time I think of it, I lift my heart in gratitude to the Lord.

(JST)

"The eyes of the LORD are on the righteous and his ears are attentive to their cry." (Ps. 34:15)

"You know the value of prayer: it is precious beyond all price. Never, never neglect it."

SIR THOMAS BUXTON

27. Unbelieving Dad

Pictures of a happy family fill photo albums from Ashley's early years and spill across her memory. Dad with his arm flung around Mom's shoulder bragging to neighbors. "Maggie was so beautiful nothing could keep me from her." Ashley remembers the way he would pause to wink at Mom and wait for her responsive smile before he continued, "I became a Christian because her dad wouldn't allow her to marry a sinner."

Up through Ashley's second-grade year, snapshots show Dad helping with the youth group at church, skiing with Mom in Vermont, and coaching his kids' soccer games under blue skies. But the year Ashley entered third grade and her mother took a job teaching at a strict Christian school, the pictures changed. Dad and Mom still posed together for photos, but Mom's eyes looked sad even when she smiled. Dad appeared sullen. Ashley vividly remembers the fight she heard coming from behind her parents' bedroom door late one night.

"They're nothing but hypocrites!" Dad shouted. "I will not attend church with a bunch of liars." Ashley couldn't quite make out Mom's words. But Dad's loud retort was impossible to miss. "I will *never* go to church again."

An electric silence hung in the air for a few moments, then the conversation continued in quieter tones. Ashley pulled the covers up to her chin, listening to the up and down murmur of her parents' voices. Mom tried to compromise, to soothe her husband's anger, but Dad's voice exploded through the door. "Attending a different church won't change anything! I don't *believe* in your God."

Then there was silence. Fear knotted in Ashley's chest. She hugged her stuffed elephant and shivered under the quilt, praying for her dad to go back to church.

But he never did. And the late night arguments continued. Life at home grew stressful.

When Dad forced them to stop praying before meals, Ashley realized her dad had completely turned his back on the Lord. Praying for his salvation became the focus of her life. She prayed for him every day—several times a day.

She wondered: If her dad could turn away from the Lord, would he turn away from her, too? But as the years passed, though he still adamantly claimed to hate the church and God, Ashley and her dad grew close. They shared a love of physical activities. They played tennis and biked together; he coached many of her sports teams.

It was her talent for running that really cemented their relationship.

Dad, a marathon runner, loved the sport as much as Ashley did. When she entered seventh grade, he took over her training. "I know we can get a track scholarship for you if you'll work hard," he encouraged her. Mom agreed.

So Ashley did work hard. Through the first three years of high school Dad helped the coach plan her workouts. She trusted Dad's instincts even more than her coach's and followed his instructions precisely. As a result she became one of the premiere high school runners in the country. Dad loved it. He cheered shamelessly for her at every meet, beaming with pride every time she broke a personal record.

Through those years, the only thing that marred the closeness she shared with her father was his continued aversion to God and church. But Ashley never stopped praying for him. Before every run, as she lay in bed in the morning, anytime she thought about her dad she prayed for him to return to God—and church.

In the summer before her senior year, Dad's prediction came true and scholarship offers began pouring in. Many big universities across the country offered a full ride for Ashley's college education.

"See! I told you this would happen if you worked hard!" Dad exclaimed. "You are gifted."

"Your dad is so proud of you," her mother told her. "I've never seen him happier."

But Ashley wasn't happy, and midway through her senior year she worked up the courage to tell her father why. "I believe God has told me to attend a Christian college," she said. "That's why I won't go to a state school."

Blood surged into her father's face, turning it an angry red. "What? You know that most Christian colleges don't offer sports scholarships. How do you plan to pay tuition?" He towered over Ashley, making her lips quiver. Finally, when she wouldn't back down he shouted, "How can you be so irresponsible?" and stomped from the room.

That night the arguments between her parents grew worse, Ashley could hear their voices behind the closed bedroom door. She heard words like "weak" and "crutch," but she couldn't hear everything. She just knew the arguments were because of her—her fault. She dropped to her knees beside her bed crying and praying once again for her father's salvation. She was convinced that if her dad knew the Lord, he wouldn't be so angry about her choice to attend a Christian university.

On New Year's Day of her senior year, her father announced his plans to move from the home. He loved his family, he said, but he did not understand them. He could no longer live with weak, irresponsible people who used God and religion as a crutch. Ashley knew he meant her.

It was the worst day of her life. Her father had left God, and now he was leaving her, too. Why hadn't God answered her prayer? If God had made her dad a Christian, as she had begged him to do for years, none of this would be happening.

The next day Ashley took her mother to a movie so they wouldn't have to watch her father move his things from the house. Mother and daughter clung to each other and sobbed through the happy ending. Guilt pressed in on Ashley. She had lost her father and caused her mother to lose the man she loved. Neither of them had any hope he would ever return.

But he came home the very next day, looking pale . . . yet strangely content.

He sank onto a kitchen chair. Ashley and her mother drew up chairs across the table from him. "Once I got to my apartment I began to see things more clearly. I realized it requires strength to take the kind of stand you took with me Ashley." Tears welled up in his eyes and Ashley began to cry, too. "Then I felt like I was being led to the Bible—drawn to it irresistibly. I didn't want to be wrong, so I fought the urge as long as I could. I watched television, arranged my furniture, and cooked. Finally I couldn't stand it any longer. I pulled out the Bible and began to read and pray."

He reached across the table and took each of their hands. "I recommitted my life to the Lord last night. I promise that from now on, we'll be a family that prays together and attends church together."

And he has kept his promise. God used Ashley's own actions to bring about the answer to her prayer.

(JST)

"Jesus . . . said, 'Go home to your family and tell them how much the Lord has done for you, and how he has had mercy on you.'" (Mark 5:19)

28. Diapering Mom

"Stop it!" Ray pushed away the flailing fists and struggled to tape his eighty-seven-year-old mother's diaper shut. "The harder you fight, the longer this will take."

"You're a nasty man!" she shrieked, and she then launched into the low tones of her endless mantra. "Help . . . Help . . . Help . . . " She continued it long after Ray finished changing her and settled her in the blue recliner. Her cries followed him into the kitchen.

"Need help with lunch, Dad?" Ray asked.

"Nope." Harold slapped the sandwich onto a plate, slipped it onto his lap, and wheeled over to the table. Elsie's cries stopped, and Ray hurried to check on her. Dad still had a mind; Mom still had legs. He found her fumbling with the front doorknob.

"Where are you going?" Ray scolded. He hated the sharp tone he heard in his voice.

"Who are you?" Elsie paused to scowl and wave a raised fist at her son. "I'll kill you."

Ray sighed. How could his sweet mother have changed into this shriveled bundle of fear and anger? She would be horrified if she knew. *Lord, this isn't fair!* he prayed. *She was a good mother, a loving mother. And I can't remember anything pleasant about her anymore. All I see is this psychotic old woman. The mother I knew doesn't deserve to be remembered like this.*

Over the next few months, an uncomplaining Ray cared for his mother and talked to God. *Will I only have miserable memories of her?* Ray asked. *Can't you help me remember some good things about her? Please? I don't want to think of her like this.*

But nothing changed. Present hard-reality trumped misty-memories. Unless he viewed the framed photos on her bureau, he couldn't even remember the way her face looked before dementia ravished her.

Two years later, Elsie died. As he made funeral arrangements, Ray redoubled his efforts to remember the love she once had for him, but he couldn't. And he couldn't feel love for her. Once again he asked the Lord to change his memories. *Can't I remember just a few good things about her?*

God answered his prayer two days before her funeral.

The family gathered around the table reminiscing. "Remember the time we camped out in that old tent at Priest Lake, and it poured?" Ray's brother asked.

The memory crashed over Ray like a giant wave. "Yeah. Mom helped Dad dig a ditch around the tent to divert the water and keep us dry." He saw her soggy clothes and wet drooping hair. "She never griped about helping her kids, did she?" Remembered love rolled over him.

"Her sweet-and-sour meatballs were amazing," his brother said.

"Oh, yeah." Ray smiled as the next wave of good memories flowed in. "But the marble cake with fudge icing . . . mmmmmm." The wave flowed back out, carrying bad memories with it.

For the rest of the afternoon, wonderful memories of the mother he loved rushed over Ray, sweeping in the good memories, carrying away the bad ones, allowing him to remember his beloved mother the way she deserved to be remembered.

(JST)

"Honor your father and mother, so that you may live long in the land the LORD your God is giving you." (Exod. 20:12)

29. Rachel's Answer

The doctor motioned Rachel into the hospital waiting room where they could speak privately. "Your son's infection has spread," he told her. "I'm afraid we're going to have to remove Nathaniel's spleen first thing in the morning."

A lump formed in Rachel's throat, and she bit her lip against tears, but she didn't question the doctor. He had to do what he had to do. "May I stay in Nathaniel's room tonight?" she asked.

The doctor granted permission, and nurses dragged a mattress from across the hall into Nathaniel's room so Rachel could sleep on the floor by her son's bed.

But Rachel slept very little. Instead, she shot brief prayers heavenward as she tended her son.

Time and time again, Nathaniel crawled out of bed and stumbled around the room in his delirium. Each time, Rachel guided him back to bed and called out for God to save his spleen and heal him.

By morning, she was too exhausted to pray any more.

But prayer had done its job. The doctors figured out an alternate way to deal with Nathaniel's problem. They did not remove his spleen. God had answered the prayers of a loving mother.

(JST)

"Ask and it will be given to you; seek and you will find; knock and the door will be opened to you." (Matt. 7:7)

"His work empowers my prayer—
my prayers release his work."

DUTCH SHEETS, *Intercessory Prayer*

30. You'll Never Get Away with It

"Who broke the vase?" I asked.

Three innocent faces gazed up at me. Three pairs of shoulders shrugged. My heart broke. Every day of their lives, I prayed for my children to love the Lord and have soft hearts; yet one of them was lying. One of them had a hard heart.

"You may be able to lie to me," I said in a last-ditch attempt to soften hearts. They were so close in age, I never seemed able to sort out who did what—and they knew it. "But God is always watching. He knows who is lying."

Three pairs of eyes grew big with concern. Three dismayed voices protested.

"I'd be scared to lie to God," I said. Three sets of eyes unblinkingly met mine. Obviously, the perpetrator wasn't going to crack.

I walked into the kitchen, my stomach churning, my eyes filling with tears—helpless to do anything more. How could my precious children have such hard hearts?

Hearing a "Rhumm, rhumm," I glanced back into the family room. Ty and Tevin made motor sounds as they ran trucks over a pillow. They had returned to their play, but Tori hadn't joined them. She stood alone on the hearth, palms pressed together in a praying position, eyes squeezed shut, lips moving in silent prayer.

Obviously, the guilty party was feeling remorse. It looked like God had answered my daily prayer. Her little heart wasn't so hard after all. Hopefully, she'd come and confess to me, too. And she did.

(JST)

"For he views the ends of the earth and sees everything under the heavens." (Job 28:24)

31. Enough Children

Jenny and Alec agreed on one thing. They did not want more children. Not under any circumstances. Not ever. Two was more than enough.

Shortly after their youngest turned four years old Jenny found the Lord and became a Christian, but a strange thing happened. God placed an immediate yearning for more children in her heart. She had no idea why, but she knew it must be from God.

When she told Alec, his response frightened her. "If you ever get pregnant, I will march you into New York City for an abortion."

She knew he meant it. So she began to pray for the Lord to change his heart. At the same time, she prayed for his salvation, excitedly reading the Bible aloud to him at every opportunity. As a result, six months after Jenny found the Lord, Alec yielded his heart to God, too.

Nevertheless, his opposition to having more children didn't change, while Jenny's longing for them grew stronger. So she kept praying about it.

One hot day, as they worked in the yard together, a desire to talk to Alec about more children pressed in on Jenny again. She knew he hadn't changed his mind and she was afraid to talk to him, but her heart felt as though it would burst if she didn't. So when they finished weeding, and tromped into the house for a glass of lemonade, Jenny cleared her throat and began. "Um, Alec . . ."

"Yes?"

"I want to talk to you about something." Jenny took a sip of her drink and prayed for courage.

"I think I already know what it is," Alec said. His voice sounded tender.

"You do?"

He smiled and reached across the glass table for her hand. "Yes. I don't understand how or why, but the Lord has put a strong desire for more children into my heart."

Jenny nearly fell off her chair.

"I think it might be fun to go start one right now," he said.

Today, Jenny and Alec are the proud parents of five children.

(JST)

"Eli answered, 'Go in peace, and may the God of Israel grant you what you have asked of him.' . . . So in the course of time Hannah conceived and gave birth to a son. She named him Samuel, saying, 'Because I asked the Lord for him.'" (1 Sam. 1:17, 20)

32. Bible Baggage

Nothing matters more to me than my children's relationship with the Lord. Nothing.

I want them to love him fervently. I pray for their spiritual health every single day. *Lord, keep their hearts right. Make them love you. Draw them to seek you with their whole beings. Make them long for your Word and diligently read their Bibles.*

The problem is, I can't know the true condition of their hearts. No one but God can know that for sure. I have to judge by the fruit I see in their lives.

And now that they all attend college or graduate school, sometimes I find myself worrying they may not read their Bibles every day. I know how busy they are with school and work. Sometimes just to reassure myself, I have an inner desire to badger them. "Do you read your Bible every day? Every single day?" But I know that offends them, so I don't. I just continue praying for them not to neglect their Bible reading—because I know staying in the Word will pull them closer to the Lord.

Still, I can't resist asking God to let me know how they are doing. And last week, God answered my prayer.

The family had flown to Illinois to visit my elderly parents for ten days. One afternoon while my parents stayed home to rest, we piled into the car for a day trip. Our three adult-children crowded into the backseat, while Ray and I sat in the front. As I leaned my head back and closed my eyes, I remembered I had read only one chapter in the Bible that morning.

"Nuts," I said. "I didn't finish reading my Bible today. Anyone got one?" I knew no one would have a copy in the small rental car.

"There are two back here," Ty said. He and Tori each held up a copy of a Bible. "Which one do you want?" My heart soared.

Four days later, at Midway Airport in Chicago, I noticed Ty and Tevin both carrying Bibles onto the plane. Were they doing it as a witness? Or because they treasured what was in it?

I'll never know, but God does. And he answered my prayer by showing me how my children constantly keep his Word near.

(JST)

"How can a young man keep his way pure? By living according to your word." (Ps. 119:9)

"Your word is a lamp to my feet and a light for my path." (Ps. 119:105)

33. Small Prayers

Most of my prayers are easy-to-overlook, small prayers. God nearly always answers them. And I nearly always overlook the answers. But I noticed an answer recently.

In the middle of the night, pain as intense as labor slammed me. Hours later, I birthed a three-millimeter kidney stone. And if that wasn't bad enough, a CAT scan showed more stones in both kidneys. Doctors pronounced me a Stone Former. Kidney stones and pain could recur again and again.

I know what you're expecting. You think I prayed for healing and for the stones to miraculously dissolve. Nope. I'm afraid the stones may be my "thorn in the flesh." God may intend for them to purify my character. I don't like that, but I accept it.

No, my prayer concerned food.

It seems that nearly anything I put in my mouth could form kidney stones. The worst culprits appeared to be the things I loved best: berries, cheese, yogurt, spinach, peanuts, even protein, which doctors limited to six ounces a day. What could I eat? And how could I stand any of it without salt?

Self-pity drove me to the Doughnut Diet. My week-long pastry binge culminated when a friend who owns a doughnut shop brought me a specially baked apple fritter so enormous it wouldn't fit on an eight-inch plate. After downing it, I felt so crummy I was ready to beg for forgiveness and ask for help.

I know sugar is one of the few things I'm allowed to eat, I told the Lord as I drifted off to sleep. *But I also know how unhealthy this kind of eating is. The problem is, I honestly can't figure out what to cook. Help me!*

The next morning when I awoke, the words "minted carrots" floated through my brain. Carrots! I hadn't eaten cooked carrots for years. Then I remembered vegetable mélange—beans and rice. Recipes and ideas for things I could eat came to mind.

The Lord answered my prayer by planning my menu.

I suppose some people might think I shouldn't bother God with details like that. I should get a cookbook and look it up for myself. But he didn't seem to mind. And I love noticing the answer to a small prayer.

(JST)

"For through me your days will be many, and years will be added to your life." (Prov. 9:11)

"God is concerned for daily details . . . We must ask about day-to-day matters as well as large eternal issues."

JACK HAYFORD, *Prayer is Invading the Impossible*

34. Not a Stranger

I customarily lapse into prayer whenever I listen to the news. I can't help it. Pictures of refugees call forth tears and pleas for God's help. Stories about house fires cause me to pray for God to comfort the victims.

So it made sense that I would pray as soon as the news anchor on our local television station showed a helicopter rescuing a man who had fallen from Larch Mountain. I couldn't see the man's face and they didn't give his name, but I prayed fervently for him that evening and the next day.

I wondered about his age and whether or not he knew the Lord, and, though my prayers for these people usually last only for the duration of the newscasts, I found myself praying for this man several times over the next few days. I asked God to save his soul if he wasn't already a Christian or bring him back if he had wandered from his faith. I asked God to heal him and comfort the family.

After a while, I went on to other things and no longer prayed for the man. I didn't think about him again until over a year later when I received a Christmas letter from a woman I'd known in high school. "Last fall our seventeen-year-old son fell from a mountain . . ." the letter began. She went on to describe their fear and pain as a helicopter life-flighted their unconscious son to a hospital. As I read the details in her letter, I realized that the man I had seen on television a year earlier was her young son.

As my friend praised the Lord for her son's emergence from a coma and subsequent return to the Lord, I thanked God for allowing my prayers to have an impact in my friend's life—even though I had no idea for whom I was praying at the time.

(JST)

"I urge then, first of all, that requests, prayers, intercession and thanksgiving be made for everyone." (1 Tim. 2:1)

35. Retiring the Television

Helen couldn't figure out why Elizabeth always complained about her husband's retirement. Helen would love the chance to spend all day every day with her husband, Paul—but he still had to work. Her friend Elizabeth must have a difficult marriage, Helen decided.

Then Paul retired . . . and turned on the television . . . and Helen understood.

There was nothing unusual about Paul watching a lot of television. During his working years, he had always turned on the set the second he arrived home from work. Helen didn't mind too much. The house stayed quiet during the day, and she enjoyed watching the news at dinnertime.

But retirement changed things. Paul would flip on the set as soon as he woke up in the morning and watch it while he drank coffee and read the newspaper for two hours. He would nap through the news at noon, then turn up the volume for the afternoon talk shows so he could chuckle over the arguing guests as he puttered in the garage.

Helen could barely stand it. She tried talking to Paul.

"Honey, could you watch the bedroom television or watch in the family room? When you turn on the one in the living room, the sound fills the whole house." She wanted to say "contaminates" the whole house, since she hated almost everything he watched, but she held her tongue. "I like to listen to music and pray. I can't do either with the television blaring."

"Sure. I didn't know it bothered you." Paul kissed her and strolled to the bedroom to watch a court show.

The next day the television played in the living room all day again. Old habits die hard. Helen had to go outside to find a quiet place to pray.

Over the months, frustration over constant noise and unacceptable programs swelled in Helen. She couldn't keep Paul from listening to trash, but she shouldn't be forced into it, too. Finally, she talked to Elizabeth about it. "Oh, that's the problem with retirement all right," Elizabeth said. "It's the television that drives me crazy."

"Why didn't you warn me?" Helen asked.

"And how would that have helped? I still haven't figured out a solution, and Dave retired four years ago. What do you plan to do about it?"

Helen sighed. "I'll try talking to him again."

And she did. She talked to him again . . . and again . . . and again. Each time, he sweetly apologized and turned off the set in the living room. The next day, it would blast through the house again. Television gripped Paul like a drug. And he wanted his drug in the living room where his wife had to listen.

Helen had no peace. Finally, she turned to the Lord in desperation. *I hate being forced to hear the drivel that spews from the television all day, Lord. It makes it almost impossible to 'take every thought captive' and keep my mind on you. I can't concentrate when I read my Bible. Help me! Get the television out of my living room!*

A few hours later, an especially offensive program drove her to talk to Paul . . . again.

"Oh, I'm sorry, sweetie. I'll watch it in the bedroom or the family room." Paul smiled and reached over to squeeze her hand. "Just tell me when it bothers you."

"It always bothers me!" Helen said. "Always, always, always!"

"Fine!" Paul jumped up angrily, and Helen regretted her sharp tone. He grabbed the heavy television and headed for the garage. "We don't have to keep it in here if you don't want it. I can put it in the garage."

Helen fought the urge to hurry after him and tell him it was okay to leave the television in the living room. Fighting always upset her. She desperately wanted to say, "I'm sorry," and make things right between them. But she held her tongue. If the Lord had chosen this way of answering her prayer, she didn't intend to do anything to interfere.

The garage door banged shut, and she heard her husband moving furniture in his workshop, probably clearing a spot for his television. She expected to feel anxious, but instead, Helen smiled. Paul's anger would disappear in a day or two, and they could watch shows they both liked in the bedroom, together. *Well, Lord,* she whispered to the quiet room, *this is certainly the strangest answer to prayer I've ever gotten.*

(JST)

"I will walk in my house with blameless heart. I will set before my eyes no vile thing." (Ps. 101:2, 3)

36. Fire under the Hood

No warning lights came on, so Karla had no way of knowing the smoke billowing from under her hood signaled an electric fire. If she had understood the danger, she would have stopped in the dark night and shooed her two children from the car. Instead, she screamed, "Pray for God to get us home safely!"

In the backseat, Katrina closed her eyes and prayed aloud, "Jesus, get us home safely."

Keegan kept his eyes open, watching the smoke as he prayed fervently, *Get us home safe, God! Please!*

All three continued to pray desperately for the next five minutes, until Karla turned the car into their driveway, and all three jumped out . . . unharmed.

Later, after the smoke cleared and the car cooled, Karla stood beside her husband as he lifted the hood and peeked underneath. His face blanched when he swept the beam of a flashlight over melted wires and blackened metal. His hand closed around hers. "God protected you."

"It was a miracle we got home safely, wasn't it?" Karla asked.

Keith nodded, then asked incredulously, "Your headlights stayed on?"

"Yes," she whispered, resting her head on his shoulder and remembering the beautiful voices of their children as they cried out to the Lord. "The headlights even stayed on."

(JST)

"Keep me safe, O God, for in you I take refuge." (Ps. 16:1)

37. Too Old?

Are you familiar with a "fleece" prayer? The Bible records that kind of prayer in the Book of Judges. God called Gideon to lead Israel into battle against the Midianites, but Gideon felt inadequate and unwilling. "My clan is the weakest and I'm the least in my family," he said. "Show me if you really plan to use me to save Israel. I'll place a wool fleece on the threshing floor. If there's dew on the fleece and the ground is dry, I'll know that you will do just as you promised." And that is what happened. Still unsure, Gideon asked God to reverse things and make the wool dry and the floor wet (see Judges 6:36–40). And God did.

An occasional fleece prayer can help encourage us in God's will. That is exactly the kind of prayer Evelyn prayed when the Holy Spirit urged her to go back to women's Bible study. She felt inadequate and argued with God, just like Gideon. *Lord, I'm eighty-two years old. All the other women at Bible study are young. They won't want an old woman like me there. What could I possibly share that would be valuable to them?* But the Holy Spirit pursued her, convicting her that Bible study was what she should do. He expected her, as an older woman, to teach the younger women. The wrestling match with God continued day in and day out.

Finally, Evelyn offered up a fleece prayer to God.

All right, Lord, she prayed. *I haven't talked to Dianne for months. I'd be shocked if she phoned. If I'm really supposed to go to the women's study, have her call me. If she phones, I'll go.* Evelyn was certain Dianne wouldn't phone. "There, that settles it, I'm off the hook," Evelyn thought.

Several more days went by, and deep conviction continued to build in Evelyn's spirit that attending Bible study was God's desire for her. *Have Dianne call me, Lord, and that will confirm I'm to go.*

Two weeks after Evelyn first prayed, her phone rang. "Come back to Bible study. We all miss you," Dianne urged. Evelyn, amazed, could hardly believe her ears!

You can guess the rest of the story. Evelyn is attending the study again, enjoying the fellowship of ladies who love her—and helping in the battle for righteousness with her seasoned wisdom.

(PP)

"Then they [older women] can train the younger women to love their husbands and children, to be self-controlled and pure, to be busy at home, to be kind, and to be subject to their husbands, so that no one will malign the word of God." (Titus 2:4, 5)

38. Details, Details, Details

Jeff worked seventy hours a week for two years as a legislative aide in Washington D.C. He loved meeting senators and observing the ins and outs of politics. He enjoyed problem solving over the phone with the people running the office in his home state. As a single male just out of college, the pace suited him. The only drawback was, he rarely got to go home.

The following year, the Lord directed Jeff to law school. He still had unmet goals in Washington—he wanted to meet the president and the people who worked in the local office in his state. But he quit his job in the senate office and plunged into his studies with a vengeance. And he loved it.

He also loved law school's Christmas break, which offered him the chance to go home for the first time in a year. One afternoon, after a week of hugging parents and playing video games with friends, Jeff strolled on a downtown street near the senate home office. He'd never met the people there, though he had spent hours chatting with them on the phone. He really wanted to meet them, to connect faces to the voices he knew so well.

But there was a problem. The president was visiting town the next day. Jeff understood the demands on the people in the local office at such a time. He remembered the panicked pace, the seventy-hour workweeks. The last thing he wanted to do was bother them.

He hesitated outside the building. Should he go up? It was a small thing, an unimportant detail, but Jeff always took details to God. *Lord,* he prayed, *is it okay for me to go up? I really want to meet everyone. If I won't be an intrusion, would you get me into the office without my doing anything to make it happen?*

He stepped aside to make way for a man loaded down with fast food. "Jeff!" The man stopped, peering over a mound of food bags.

"Tom!" Jeff laughed, recognizing a fellow worker from the Washington office. "I'd shake your hand, Tom, but I might dump your burgers."

"Yeah. Lunch for the bunch." Tom grimaced, then smiled. "Everyone's too busy to leave the office." He started walking rapidly again, gesturing with his head for Jeff to follow. "Come on up. Everyone from the D.C. office is here helping the locals prepare for the president's visit. They'd kill me if I didn't bring you up to say hi."

Upstairs in the office, Jeff chatted with all the coworkers he had missed since he left the D.C. job. He met the local people he'd wanted to meet for so long. And—one last fun detail—Tom handed him a ticket to meet the president of the United States on the following day.

Jeff is young, but he understands something many mature Christians never do. God delights in us. He loves us to hold the details of our lives up to him. And when we do, he often gives us more than we ask for.

(JST)

"The steps of the godly are directed by the LORD. He delights in every detail of their lives." (Ps. 37:23 NLT)

"You need not cry very loud: he is nearer to us than we think."

BROTHER LAWRENCE

39. The Prayer God Always Answers Yes

Spencer was a pastor's son voted most likely to succeed in high school. But by age twenty-nine, with two divorces behind him and a third marriage on the rocks, he thought of himself as anything but a success. He was a miserable failure who had no idea how to handle life. Totally sickened by himself, he considered suicide. But he didn't do it.

Instead, filled with remorse, he bowed his heart before the Lord, confessing his sins. *I am so sorry. Please forgive me*, he prayed. *Come into my heart and be Lord of my life. If you'll show me the right way to live, I will obey you.*

God answered Spencer's plea for forgiveness and salvation with a resounding "Yes." He completely changed Spencer and healed his marriage.

Though these particular details tell Spencer's story, every Christian who has ever lived has had a similar one. We all felt remorse for our sins. Then we came in faith to Jesus for forgiveness. God will always answer each of us with a yes, and then, begin the healing process.

If this story isn't your story yet, it can be. When you arrive at a point of great sorrow over your sins, when you know you need help ordering your life, turn to Jesus. He will answer yes and create you anew.

(JST)

"Therefore, if anyone is in Christ, he is a new creation; the old has gone, the new has come!" (2 Cor. 5:17)

40. Three Bedrooms Upstairs

Paige lowered her pregnant bulk into the turtle-shaped kiddy pool and rested a newspaper on her head to protect her face from the summer sun. "Matt, don't push your brother so high," she yelled across the yard's tall grass to her sons playing on the rickety swing set she had found at a garage sale.

With a sigh, she unscrewed the lid from a brown-plastic bottle and smeared #30 suntan lotion over her shoulders and arms. Even with the lotion protecting her, she was bound to burn today. She'd spent too much time in the sun, but she couldn't bear one more second in the rental house smelling of the urine-soaked carpet. Without air conditioning, the odor seemed to rise up and thicken as the summer days progressed.

Matt and JR wandered over and crawled into the tepid water with her.

"Can me and JR have a Popsicle, Mommy?" Matt asked. He smacked the water with the flat of his hand. "We're really hot."

"Sure. Bring me one, too, will you?" Paige asked.

Through the sliding door she watched her son stand on tiptoe to open the freezer over the refrigerator. "Bring me the phone, will you, honey?" she called out. Matt closed the freezer and lifted the hand-set off the receiver.

Paige dialed her friend while her sons wandered back to the swings with their frozen treats. "I can't stand much more, Shirley." Paige sucked raspberry flavor from her Popsicle. "I've been sitting in this stupid pool trying to stay cool, praying for a house, for three and a half months. I don't understand why God hasn't answered." A lump rose in her throat and she fought back tears of frustration. "The baby will be here in a few weeks. I don't want to live in this dirty, germ-filled, stinky rental with a newborn."

She couldn't hold back the tears any more.

"Get dressed," Shirley said. "I'll be there in half an hour and we'll pray for you to find the right house."

Forty-five minutes later, Paige and the boys lounged in Shirley's air-conditioned van.

"You ready to pray?" Shirley asked.

"Sure, but you know I've already prayed for a house," Paige said. "I pray every single day."

"I know, but have you prayed specifically for what you want?"

"I don't think what I want exists. Wade and I agree we want five acres. But all the houses with five acres are old fixer-uppers. We both want something new and clean."

"You need to tell God specifically what you want."

Paige rested her head on the cool headrest and closed her eyes. Both boys had already fallen asleep in the back. None of them were sleeping very well in the hot rental house. "You want a description of my dream house?"

Shirley smiled. "Yes. Tell me exactly what you'd choose if you could have anything you wanted."

Immediately, Paige rattled off the house she'd already imagined many times. "I want four bedrooms, three baths, a family room, a country kitchen, and a laundry room with a door I can close so no one will know when I haven't folded the boys underwear." She flashed a smile at her friend. "Oh, I want three of the bedrooms upstairs. And I'd love a tri-level."

"You don't want much!" Shirley laughed. "Now if you can close your eyes without dropping off to sleep, we're going to pray for God to send you that house."

"Let's do it," Paige said.

"Think it through for a minute more. Is that everything you want?"

"I want to move in before the baby comes," Paige said.

"Okay. Now let's pray," said Shirley, and the two friends bowed their heads. That afternoon, the two friends prayed for Paige's dream house, then scoured the countryside for it. They found nothing.

The next morning, Paige's phone rang. "I found a for-sale-by-owner ad in the paper and it looks promising," Shirley told her. "Let's go look at it."

A quick trip revealed it was the home the friends had agreed for in prayer the day before—a five-year-old tri-level on five acres, four bedrooms (three of them upstairs), a family room, three baths, a country kitchen, and a laundry room with a door that closed. Every detail fit Paige's and Shirley's prayer exactly.

After a few days of dickering over price, Paige and Wade signed the papers and moved in—three weeks before the birth of the baby.

(JST)

"Unless the Lord builds the house, its builders labor in vain." (Ps. 127:1)

41. The Check Is in the Mail

Martha stepped away from her ironing board and rested a hand on her swollen belly. "This time next month, little one, you'll be here," she whispered. She felt the baby move. "And I refuse to worry about how your daddy and I will pay your doctor." She looked through the window toward the heavens. *Lord, you've provided before. I trust you to do it again.*

She heard the bedroom door behind her open and glanced around expectantly. Her husband crossed the room, a stack of envelopes in his hand and concern etched on his face. "Honey, we don't have the money to pay our bills." He showed her his sheet of careful calculations. Sure enough, the money they had received didn't cover their ninety-dollar monthly expenses.

As home missionaries, Martha and Lester organized Sunday schools in poor, rural areas of the United States. They lived by faith, existing on the money sent them by fellow Christians who supported their work.

"Let's pray about it," said Lester, dropping to his knees beside an armchair. Martha carefully lowered herself into the seat and reached for her husband's hand, determined not to fear but to trust God to provide for them. She prayed, *Father, we know you love us and care about each detail of our lives . . .*

The jangling of the phone interrupted their prayer time. Lester reached over and picked up the receiver, listened, then responded, "Yes." After a few more moments, he replaced the receiver and rocked back on his heels, a bewildered look on his face.

"What was that all about?" Martha asked.

"It was Western Union," he said. "They read a telegram."

Martha tried to ignore the rush of anxiety his words brought. "It's not bad news, is it?"

Lester shook his head. "It's from my navy buddy, Steve. He's sending a hundred dollars."

Stunned, Martha said, "A hundred dollars? But you haven't seen Steve since your navy days. How would he know our address?"

"Beats me. How would he even know we needed money?" Then a grin spread across Lester's face and he quoted, "Before they call I will answer; and while they are still speaking I will hear. Isaiah . . ."

"65:24," Martha finished for him. She felt breathless as the significance of the news sunk in. "Lester, that hundred dollars will cover the bills and give us extra money for the baby!" Gratefulness flooded her heart. She smiled at her husband. "Isn't God good?"

"He sure is," her husband responded. "But I'd give my eye teeth to know how he pulled this one off."

Several days earlier, Steve awoke in the middle of the night, the impression of a dream still strong in his mind. In his dream, he heard God's voice telling him to send one hundred dollars to Colorado. And he didn't want to do it. Lying on his bed in the dark, he argued with God. *That's my savings, Lord. I'm not in the Navy earning money anymore. I'm a Bible school student—remember?*

He turned over and tried to sleep, but the dream nagged at him. Finally, he prayed, *God that hundred dollars is for next year's tuition and expenses. If you really want me to do this, send the dream a second time.* Feeling guilty about testing God but sure this was the end of the matter, Steve drifted into an uneasy sleep.

The dream recurred.

The next morning he knelt by his bed, convicted and awestruck that God would send the dream a second time. *I get the message, Lord, and I'm sorry I didn't listen the first time. But you'll have to show me where to send the money because I don't know a soul in Colorado.*

Steve spent the next few days pondering his dilemma, praying for an answer. Walking through the school lobby one afternoon, he heard a familiar voice call out, "Steve! Long time, no see."

Steve turned to see Dawson Trotman, who conducted Bible studies for Navy seamen and later founded the Navigators. "Daws! What are you doing here?"

His friend and mentor caught up with him. "Following up on some of my guys."

Steve pounded Dawson on the back. "It's great to see you. What have you been doing?"

"I've just come back from Colorado. Visited Martha and Lester."

Steve stopped in his tracks. "They live in Colorado?" He shot a prayer heavenward. *God, is this the answer to my prayer?* "Do they need money?" he asked Dawson.

Dawson shrugged. "They didn't say anything, but Martha's baby is due in a month."

Steve exclaimed, "It has to be them!" He glanced at his watch. "Listen, Daws, I have to be in class in ten minutes. I can't explain right now, but I need to take care of this immediately. Will you send a telegram for me?"

Sixty-two years later, that telegram resides in Carolyn Spencer Hopkin's baby book, a tribute to one man's obedience and God's faithfulness to provide for his children. The telegram reads: "$100 gift for Martha forthcoming. Phil. 4:19. Steve."

(BM)

"And my God will meet all your needs according to his glorious riches in Christ Jesus." (Phil. 4:19)

42. I'll Have the Special Fruit Plate

An idea popped into Darcey's head somewhere between changing dirty diapers and reading *Red Fish, Blue Fish* for the hundredth time. "Wouldn't it be fun to concoct my elaborate fruit platter for Millie?" Darcey didn't know if her elderly neighbor would want the salad, but she felt a strong urge to make it.

"Honey," she snuggled up on the couch by her husband and rested her head on his shoulder, "would you watch the boys while I run to the grocery store and buy some fruit for that fancy salad I make?"

"We like your canned peaches better," he said without looking up from the sports page.

"I'm so glad!" She jumped up and grabbed the car keys. "Because we're having peaches with dinner tonight. I'm making the fruit platter for Millie."

Pushing her cart through the rows of fresh produce, Darcey smiled, anticipating her elderly friend's response. At the sight of the salad, Millie's eyes would grow wide, and she'd gasp with delight. This was so much fun!

Back at home, while her husband's lawnmower grumbled in the backyard, Darcey loaded her purchases onto the center of the kitchen table, and both boys watched—elbows on the table, fists under chins. Darcey peeled a cantaloupe, cut a hole in the top, scooped out the seeds, then helped Dana frost it with cream cheese and roll it in coconut.

Two-year-old Carson climbed up on a chair and stretched the upper half of his body across the flat surface of the table. "It wooks wike a giant snowball, Mommy."

Darcey smiled and kissed the top of his head, then placed the cantaloupe in the center of a huge glass platter. "Okay, Dana, you show Carson how to fill the hole in the middle with strawberries and grapes while I scoop out some watermelon balls."

A few minutes later, Carson said, "We're wokking haud."

Darcey laughed. "Yes we are. I don't think I'd go to this much trouble for anyone but Millie. I'd just take them a jar of my canned peaches."

They finished by piling mounds of fruit around the "snowball" and edging the whole platter with mint leaves from the garden. Then Darcey lifted it up for everyone to admire.

"It wooks wike a picture fwom a magazine!" Carson said.

"You should be an artist, Mommy," Dana told her.

It really did look like a work of art. Millie would love it.

"Okay, guys. Go tell Daddy I said to watch you while I run this over to Millie."

Darcey settled the plastic-wrapped salad on the passenger seat and started down the driveway. As she turned into the street, she suddenly thought, "I should take the salad to Wanda."

The thought startled her. "No!" she said out loud. "Why would I think something like that? I wouldn't go to this much trouble for anyone but Millie. She's done so many things for me."

The thought returned, unbidden. "Take the salad to Wanda."

"I don't want to!" The intensity of her response startled her. "I've been looking forward to giving it to Millie all morning."

"Take it to Wanda."

The conviction that God was speaking closed around her. She sighed with resignation, willing to obey but unable to completely push away her disappointed, angry feelings. She would never have made the salad if she'd known it was for Wanda. Stepping on the gas, she passed Millie's house without even glancing sideways.

At Wanda's, she pasted a fake smile on her face and rang the doorbell. When Wanda pulled open the door, Darcey placed the platter in her hands, saying simply, "This is for you."

Wanda stared at Darcey dumbfounded for a moment, then stared at the platter. She said nothing. She seemed to have forgotten all about Darcey.

Darcey shifted uncomfortably, unable to read Wanda's expression. Was Wanda upset with her? Maybe God had not spoken to her after all.

"Give Wanda five dollars."

Surprised by an unexpected thought for the second time in half an hour and realizing she couldn't look any more foolish than she already did, Darcey reached into her purse. She pulled out a five-dollar bill and held the money toward Wanda, fully expecting the other woman to take offense and refuse it.

Instead, Wanda balanced the fruit platter in her right hand so she could hold the money with her left. As she glanced back and forth from the salad to the money, she began to cry. "Did you know my husband lost his job last month?"

"No!"

"And we have a Japanese student staying with us." Wanda met Darcey's eyes for the first time. "Can you come in for a minute?"

Darcey followed Wanda to the kitchen. Wanda set two mugs on the table, then sat in a chair across from Darcey. "Everything has gone wrong lately." Her eyes stared vacantly into the distance. "Last week things got so bad I decided it doesn't do any good to follow the Lord."

"Oh Wanda . . . " Darcey's hand involuntarily fluttered to her mouth.

"Let me finish." Wanda held up her hand. "Two days ago I found out we have to take our Japanese student to a picnic tonight. They told me to bring a salad." Tears pooled in her eyes. "I didn't have money for a salad or gas to get there, so I told God, *If you're really there, God, and if you care about me, send me a salad and give me money for gas. I decided if he did it, I'd give him another chance.*

Tears slid down Wanda's cheeks. "I wasn't even nice to him about it. I didn't think he could do it." The teakettle squealed, and Wanda jumped up to grab it, then stood holding the steaming pot, gazing at Darcey's face. "But he heard my prayer. He sent you with a salad and gas money." She giggled through her tears and nodded toward the fruit platter on her counter. "And that has to be the most fabulous salad on the face of the earth!"

For the next hour, the two women shared tea, tears, and laughter. "It doesn't matter which end of a prayer you're on," Darcey told Wanda before they parted. "When God answers, it feels great."

(JST)

"Now to Him who is able to do exceedingly abundantly above all that we ask or think, according to the power that works in us, to Him be glory in the church." (Eph. 3:20–21 NKJV)

43. I'd Like a White One, Please!

"We can't leave the refrigerator in the kitchen. It's leaking," Ginni told her four kids. "We'll end up with dry rot under the linoleum. We're going to have to push it out to the garage."

Fourteen-year-old Jon crossed his arms. "You mean we have to go clear out to the garage for milk?"

Ginni pretended a cheerfulness she didn't feel. "Sure! It's just a few feet further."

"Why don't we get a new one?" Jon prodded. Did her oldest son know how badly she felt about her inability to provide for her four children? Her job teaching at a Christian school barely put food on the table.

"You know I've looked in the paper for a refrigerator for over a year." She sopped up the puddle in front of the fridge with a stained pink towel. "Even if we could afford one, we couldn't afford to pay someone to haul this one away." She hadn't expected Bob to quit his job and stop paying child support.

Jon grimaced and headed for the door. "I'll borrow the neighbor's dolly."

Half an hour later, the refrigerator slumped in the garage next to the kitchen door, plugged in, and already oozing liquid onto the cement floor. "Thanks for the help, guys!"

Ginni shooed the kids back into the house and arranged an armful of rags around the refrigerator's base. Through the closed door that led to the house, she could hear the muffled theme song of the kids' favorite sitcom. She leaned against the hood of her old car, head down, hugging herself and crying.

Lord, I can't do this. I can't take care of four kids by myself. Will you help me? In the year since the refrigerator started going bad, had she ever asked the Lord for a new one? She couldn't remember. Okay, she'd ask. *I need a refrigerator, Lord.* She remembered someone saying prayers should be specific. *And I need someone who will cart this one off and deliver the new one. It can be used, but I'd really like a nice one.* Ginni liked pretty things. *And could you make it white to match the stove?*

The next afternoon, the father of one of her students poked his head into her empty classroom. "Mrs. Ellett?"

Ginni glanced up from her paper grading to see the owner of Swanson Appliances, "How are you, Mr. Swanson?"

"Remember about a year ago when you asked me if I had a refrigerator?" He stepped into the classroom, holding the door open with his foot. "Do you still need one?"

"Yes." Ginni could feel her pulse throbbing in her throat.

"Well, I got one in, and I'll give it to you—if you want it. It's used, but it's nice. And it's free."

"Oh, I . . ." Ginni searched for words.

He must have gotten the impression she didn't want it, because he quickly added, "I'll deliver it and get rid of that old one for you."

"Thank you!" Ginni stood and hurried over to shake his hand. "I'm so grateful!"

"I'll bring it this evening if that's okay with you. About seven?"

"That would be wonderful, Mr. Swanson." He turned to leave. "Mr. Swanson?"

"Yes?" He looked at her again.

"What color is it?" she asked.

"White." Concern furrowed his brow. "Is that all right?"

"It's more than all right," Ginni said with a smile. "It's exactly what I wanted."

(JST)

"A father to the fatherless, a defender of widows, is God in his holy dwelling." (Ps. 68:5)

44. Don't Pray This

Lord, I don't care what it looks like. I just want a house, I prayed foolishly.

God answered! And boy, did he answer—the exact prayer I'd prayed. All I could do was shake my head in disbelief. But . . .

We could afford it. So, we bought it. Everything was in disrepair; it was an old house with small rooms. Unlived in for months, the walls were so dusty I had to vacuum them before I could start painting. We needed new carpet, new drapes, and new linoleum. The kitchen sink hit me at least six inches below my hips. Had a vertically challenged family lived here?

Outdoors, we sanded and scraped, and sanded and scraped, and sanded . . . you get the idea, before painting. The looooooooong redwood fence soaked up enough redwood stain to fill a large swimming pool—brushed on by hand, of course, because my father-in-law didn't offer his paint sprayer until I was finished.

As soon as possible, we fixed everything, except the kitchen sink, and moved elsewhere. It turned out perfectly; the next buyer was a short woman.

I never prayed that prayer again. We've lived in several other homes, all lovely. I pray very specific prayers these days. (PP)

"But seek first his kingdom and his righteousness, and all these things will be given to you as well." (Matt. 6:33)

45. Tears in the Throne Room

Nora knelt in front of the basement toilet, sopping up the foul overflow with her best towels. She had snatched them from the upstairs linen closet when Anna yelled that the commode downstairs was flooding again.

"Mom, aren't those the good towels?" Anna asked from the doorway.

Lifting a dripping towel, Nora squeezed the water into a green five-gallon bucket. Her stomach revolted at the stench, and for a moment she thought she might upchuck.

"Are you okay, Mom?" Anna asked.

"I'm fine, honey," Nora assured her. "I'm just upset about the toilet. Why don't you go upstairs and watch Seth for me. Okay?"

"Okay."

As soon as she heard Anna take the stairs two at a time, Nora surrendered to the turmoil in her heart and allowed the tears to flow. She couldn't afford to ruin her good towels. She couldn't afford rubber gloves to protect her hands from the germ-laden, nasty mess. She couldn't afford to have a toilet flooding her basement bedroom the day before their new roommate moved into it. As a single mom with three kids and a husband who wouldn't pay child support, she needed that rent money.

And she'd already paid through the nose for a plumber to fix this toilet which continued to flood. Obviously, she'd wasted that much-needed cash.

Lord, I don't think I've ever prayed for a toilet before, Nora said. *But this one needs help. And so do I. I can't rent this room if the toilet keeps flooding. And I have to have the extra money I'll get from rent.*

Scrubbing the floor with pine cleaner to cover the odor and kill the germs, she continued to pray. *I don't know what to do! Help me!*

Later that day, Ellis Cookman, a plumber whose kids attended the same school as her kids, showed up unexpectedly at her door.

"You got a toilet that's crying out for help?" he joked.

Nora had no idea how he knew, but she gratefully led him to the basement and pointed out the offender. Ellis knelt over it, uncoiling the biggest plumber's snake she'd ever seen.

After a few minutes, he announced, "Yep, there's somethin' down there all right, but I can't get it. I'm going to have to pull the toilet." Ten minutes later, with the commode sitting in the tub, Ellis yanked a foot-long piece of wood as big around as Nora's arm out of the hole. Wrinkling his nose, he held it up for her to see. "Phew! There's your problem."

"Oh, my goodness!" Nora exclaimed. "Does this mean the toilet is fixed?"

"Well, actually, that toilet of yours is beyond fixing." He pointed at a crack running vertically up the tank. "But I've got a 'new' one in the truck I carried out of a remodel this morning. Care if we trade 'thrones'?" His eyes twinkled.

For the next half-hour, Nora and her children shook their heads in disbelief and wonder as Ellis installed a beautiful toilet in their basement bathroom. God had not only answered Nora's prayer, he had given her more than she asked for.

(JST)

"For he will deliver the needy who cry out, the afflicted who have no one to help." (Ps. 72:12)

46. Windy Business

When Roald sold his manufacturing company and invested in windmills, he expected enormous success. After all, as an engineer with a master's degree, he'd always done well in business, and wind energy was the up-and-coming thing. But a year passed, money ran low, and he still hadn't sold a single one of the wind machines he purchased as a start-up.

He tried everything. He called potential customers. No one saw the need to buy a windmill. He organized a seminar attended by several wealthy investors and charmed the attendees with his best selling techniques; no one took the bait. He had expected the seminar to pull in money, but it ended up as one more sheet on the pile of expenses. The one-and-a-half-million-dollar debt he had incurred to finance the windmills loomed like a dark mountain directly ahead of him.

"I've tried everything I know how to do," he told his wife.

"Exactly how long until the loan is due?" Ginger asked.

"Three-and-a-half weeks." Roald ran his fingers through his hair, then rested his elbows on the jumble of papers littering the mahogany table and buried his face in his hands.

"Then what?"

Roald shrugged. "Bankruptcy. WindLand is finished." He had no idea what he'd do to support the family.

"Surely, there's something . . ."

"There's nothing! I've run out of ideas!" Instantly, Roald regretted his sharp tone and reached for Ginger's hand. "Sorry. It's just . . ."

"I know." She wrapped her arms around his neck and rested her head on top of his head. Her touch and smell comforted him.

"Hey!" Suddenly, Ginger drew back to look at him. "What time it is?"

Her change in tone amused him; he glanced at his watch. "6:49. Why?"

"We told the pastor's wife we'd pray for the pregnant lady at church who's having trouble sleeping. Remember?"

He didn't remember. "Is this someone we know?"

"No."

"And we're praying for her because . . . "

"Because the pastor's wife organized round-the-clock prayer for her, and we promised to pray between seven and eight tonight."

"We're supposed to pray for an hour?"

Ginger giggled. "We can do it. Remember that time we prayed for five minutes?"

Roald laughed. "Well, we can try. It beats sitting around worrying. Do we have to kneel for the whole hour?"

"I don't know."

By the time seven o'clock rolled around, they had decided they should kneel. So they did. Then, after their knees started to hurt and turn red, they agreed it would be okay to sit on the couch and hold hands as they prayed. Surprisingly, they actually stayed in prayer for the entire sixty minutes as God led them in precise ways to pray for a woman they'd never met and knew little about.

The next morning, the pastor's wife called to announce that the pregnant woman slept through the night and was feeling much better.

When Ginger reported how quickly their prayers had been answered, Roald asked, "Why haven't we ever prayed for our business?"

"I don't know." She spoke slowly, looking thoughtful.

"Want to try it when I get home from work tonight?"

"Sure."

And that is exactly what they did. After dinner they spent another hour in prayer. Only this time they prayed for God to make their business successful. When they finished, Roald felt a peace about the business he'd never felt before. He felt God saying, "I'm in charge, not you. The business is my responsibility, not yours. Just trust me."

The next morning, Roald approached work with joy in his heart. He relaxed and chatted in his office with the man who had purchased his manufacturing company a year earlier. The phone rang and Roald answered.

"Yes?"

"Do you have any of those windmills left?" asked a doctor from Orange County who had attended Roald's seminar months earlier.

"Windmills? Maybe one or two," said Roald.

The man in Roald's office leaned forward in his chair, obviously piqued by the conversation. It was the first time he had indicated an interest in the windmills, though Roald had tried to convince him several times that he needed one.

"I'd like to buy one, and I have a couple of friends who are interested, too," said the doctor. Before the conversation ended, Roald wrote up a contract to sell four.

"I might be interested in a couple of those wind machines," the man in Roald's office said when Roald hung up the phone. "Do you have any left?"

"I do," Roald said.

Before two weeks passed, he could no longer say that—because by then, he had sold every single windmill in WindLand's inventory.

Twenty years later, he and Ginger still give God all the glory for his miraculous provision. With God, circumstances are never hopeless.

(JST)

"Walk in all the way that the LORD your God has commanded you, so that you may live and prosper and prolong your days in the land that you will possess." (Deut. 5:33)

"God will do nothing on earth except in answer to believing prayer."

JOHN WESLEY

47. Just Thinking

Several years ago, Faith suspected her husband of sexually abusing her two young daughters. No eyewitnesses stepped forward, of course, but the circumstantial evidence proved overwhelming. She separated from him to protect her girls, raising her children alone.

Her husband withdrew all financial support. Her job paid poorly. She claimed Isaiah 54:5 as her special verse, "For your Maker is your husband." She begged the Lord to walk beside her . . . and be her husband.

Faith went through some difficult times. One day she left the grocery store with only a bag of potatoes to feed her family of five. Nevertheless, during that period, she felt the Lord's presence with her. When she leaned on him for help, he seemed to supply every need the second she thought about it.

Once she thought, "Wouldn't it be nice to have a child gate for the top of the stairs so I wouldn't have to watch the baby every second?" It appeared the next day.

She thought, "I wish I could afford some new clothes." A friend brought hand-me-downs from Nordstrom's, the most expensive department store in the city.

Another time (and she's not sure if this one counts because he thought of it first) her brother said, "Faith, you need some new silverware." He riffled through her drawer, holding up different styles of "junkware" before tossing them back in disgust. She smiled and agreed with him, "Wouldn't new silverware be nice?"

That evening, her next-door neighbor sent over a twelve-piece set of antique silverware—not stainless-steel flatware, but actual silverware—in a wooden box. Nicer than she could have ever imagined.

Faith believes God walked with his arm around her in those days. He was her husband, anticipating her needs and supplying them . . . because he loved her.

(JST)

"For your Maker is your husband—the LORD Almighty is his name." (Isa. 54:5)

48. Deerly Beloved

When the engineering company Darren worked for downsized, he and his wife decided he would support the family by consulting while he looked for work. He had no difficulty finding customers, but he did have trouble collecting the money they owed him.

When things got bad, the cupboards stood empty. They didn't know how they would feed the children, so the couple knelt to beg God for help.

The next morning, a hunter friend called to offer the deer he had just recently shot. By the next evening, Darren's freezer was stuffed with venison.

(JST)

"Give us today our daily bread." (Matt: 6:11)

49. Mine, Yours, and Hours

Janie and Dave fought her cancer the way they did everything, together, leaning on God for answers and strength to meet the test. Dave grew more tender as Janie grew more needy. Ice water from downstairs? Bedpan emptied? Backrub? "I'm here for you, honey. Don't worry," he'd murmur. She prepared her body for surgery and chemotherapy; he provided for her emotional and physical support. Nothing kept Dave from Janie's side. Hospice and multitudes of friends tried to relieve him, but it didn't last long. "I just can't stand to be away from her. Besides, I know how she likes things done," he explained.

Dave used every hour of earned vacation days and sick leave—seven weeks worth—to be with her. *Oh God, I'm out of accrued time, and we desperately need my salary for bills. I've got to go back to work. What do I do? Janie needs me now more than ever. Please help us.*

The following Monday morning, Dave walked in the door at work to an incredible surprise, the kind that stuns the receiver because generosity and kindness so perfectly meet the need.

His coworkers gathered around and clapped him on the back. "We've put some of our vacation hours and sick leave into your account," one said. "Go home and be with Janie."

Two hundred and eighty-three hours, to be exact, giving him another seven weeks to spend at home with his wife, fully paid.

Dave broke into tears of joy and gratitude. " It's nothing, Dave," they insisted. "You'd do the same for us."

But it was something, a gift of precious time—moments Dave and Janie wouldn't have except for the sacrificial love of friends.

(PP)

"A friend loves at all times, and a brother is born for adversity." (Prov. 17:17)

50. Wood You Believe

Jan lay in a hospital bed in the upstairs bedroom of the home she shared with her husband, Paul. She was battling brain cancer. I'd come to encourage her and pray, but as usual, she was cheering me. "Do you know what God did for us this week?" she said with a smile.

Munching on fresh blueberries, Jan shared her story. "Earlier this fall, Paul said he'd need to order wood for the winter, but we were broke." Jan's long battle with cancer had been a financial black hole for the family. Trying to keep up with bills was impossible.

I glanced around the room at the clutter of sickness surrounding Jan. Wadded Kleenex, an assortment of books, fading flowers, and a large array of Walt Disney movies lay stacked on the table beside her bed. Though she was middle-aged, the movies brought laughter on dark days when the symptoms of her brain cancer overwhelmed her ability to cope. "When Paul first mentioned firewood, God gave me a strong impression that he would provide, that I was not to worry. So I didn't think anymore about our need for wood."

"Weeks later, I was surprised when Paul remarked again that he really had to get some wood." Jan grinned, struggling to turn over in bed. "I thought the wood was already stacked in the shed. Of course, I told him not to buy any, that God had promised me firewood. I did wonder, though, why it hadn't been delivered."

Jan's eyes seemed lit from within. Her words tumbled over each other in rapid succession. "A few days after my conversation with Paul, a friend came to visit, and I shared the firewood story with her. 'Oh no,' she confessed, red-faced. 'I'm so sorry. When some extra money was available to me, I knew God wanted me to give it to you and Paul for wood. I wrote you a check, but it's still on my desk. I thought you'd be embarrassed if I offered to pay for your wood.' "

The firewood did arrive and burned warm and bright all winter. But Jan's faith and courage shone brightest of all for me. She made me think of the sign I see advertising "seasoned firewood" near our home. Webster's dictionary says to be "seasoned" is to "make more usable." Jan's illness has "seasoned" her. Her faith has been under fire, but she has warmed and illumined many with her grace, even as the gift of wood warmed her that cold winter.

(PP)

"Yet it was good of you to share in my troubles." (Phil. 4:14 NIV)

"God can work wonders if he can get a suitable man. Men can work wonders if they can get God to lead them."

E. M. BOUNDS, *Power through Prayer*

51. Going, Going, Gone!

Keith's truck broke down, and the mechanic pronounced it beyond repair. Keith searched the newspapers for a vehicle. Nothing. The two thousand dollars he had to spend for a truck that could haul his painting equipment from place to place wasn't enough. Without transportation, Keith couldn't work and support his family. Trying not to panic, he and his wife took the problem to God.

A short time later, Keith located a half-ton, pumpkin-colored Chevy van with ladder racks at an auction he'd read about in the newspaper. Perfect . . . if the price was right and he could figure out how to bid. He'd never been to an auction before and couldn't understand a word of auctioneers' chatter.

The day of the auction, Keith sat alone in the crowd. Fear gripped him when the pumpkin-colored van came onto the auction block. He prayed fervently for the Lord to show him what to do. As soon as the bidding began, with sweat beading his brow, he raised his hand. The auctioneer indicated Keith's bid and rattled on. Keith didn't know whether to try and bid again or not. What would happen if he exceeded the two thousand dollars in his pocket? He decided to wait it out and trust God.

Finally, the auctioneer shouted, "Sold!" and pointed at Keith, the only bidder.

At the cashier window, Keith learned how much he had bid for the van—fifteen hundred dollars. He also learned it had only twenty-five thousand city miles on it. God had provided a vehicle with a great engine and left money in Keith's pocket.

(JST)

"Make it your ambition to lead a quiet life, to mind your own business and to work with your hands, just as we told you." (1 Thess. 4:11)

52. Nineteen Seventy-Three

Twenty-one-year-old Lee Newcom stepped back, stunned. "It can't be true!" Everything in him wanted to reject the words coming from his fourteen-year-old sister's mouth, but he knew from Teresa's tear-streaked face that it was true. Karen, the youth pastor's sixteen-year-old daughter was pregnant. The father-to-be was the pastor's fifteen-year-old son, Alan.

"Promise you won't tell!"

"Teresa, if Karen's pregnancy test comes back positive, they won't be able to keep it a secret for long."

"I only told you, Lee, because I feel I can trust you." Teresa's eyes filled again, pleading with him. "Nobody knows except Alan, Karen, and me. If you say anything to anyone, they'll know I told."

Lee buried his face in his hands, massaging his forehead and temples. When this news came out, he knew it could destroy both families. Worse, it could rip their small Bible church apart. To make matters worse, Alan's dad was Lee's pastor and his mentor. Lee knew he had a responsibility to tell him eventually.

Suddenly, an unexpected urgency to fast and pray flooded Lee. He knew, beyond any doubt, his only job was to pray to "the conclusion of the matter." It wasn't his job to tell anyone now. Instead, he had to pray against something Satan was trying to destroy.

Teresa's voice broke into his thoughts. "You can't tell!"

"Okay," Lee agreed, his voice thick with grief. "I won't."

Over the next three days, Lee fasted and prayed fervently. He prayed for unity in the church. He prayed for the two pastors' families. And the whole time, the importance of praying to "the conclusion of the matter" kept swirling around his brain. He knew God wanted him to pray until something ended. He assumed that meant he should pray until the news broke in the church or until Karen's and Alan's families found out or . . .

But nothing happened.

After going without food for four days, Lee broke his fast. He felt like a failure. He'd been too weak to fast to "the conclusion of the matter" as the Lord had instructed.

Five weeks later, the church learned about the pregnancy, and Karen and Alan asked for forgiveness. Rather than the turmoil and division Lee had expected, the church pulled together. Lee thought maybe his fervent prayer had helped, but he couldn't be sure.

After the birth, Karen gave the baby up for adoption. Soon, the two families moved, lost contact with each other, and the kids finished growing up.

Time passed. Karen and Alan married other people and formed two Christian families. Lee also married and had children. But the guilt over his failure to fast to "the conclusion" of anything haunted him. For years he wondered why his first attempt at fasting had failed to make an impact . . . until his phone rang in the early months of 2001.

"Lee! It's Alan. Remember me?"

"Alan! Of course, I remember you. Your dad keeps me updated a couple times a year. How are you, man?"

"I am so great you wouldn't believe it. I heard from Terri! She found me!"

"Who?"

"You know, the baby. Her adopted parents named her Terri."

It took a few seconds for the words to sink in. The baby? The baby that Alan and Karen had given up for adoption had located Alan?

On the other end of the line, Alan laughed. "Took you by surprise, huh?"

"Yes."

"You're not as shocked as I was when she first e-mailed me."

"She found you?"

"Yes. On the web. She found Karen in California, too. We talked on the phone for three hours, then I sent her a plane ticket to visit me here in Washington. She is really something, Lee. Really something! She's smart, and she's a Christian!"

"A Christian?"

"She is! We didn't know it, but a Christian couple adopted her. Is that incredible or what?"

Lee listened in amazement as Alan told him about Terri. She was married and was now a youth leader in her church.

She had been thrilled to find both her birth parents walking with the Lord.

"Can I forward you the e-mails we've exchanged over the past few months?" Alan asked Lee. "That'll give you a better picture."

"I'd like that," Lee said.

Soon after they hung up, the e-mail messages popped up in Lee's computer. As he read them, the part of Alan's story he'd never known before unfolded. A lump formed in his throat.

Alan's e-mails to Terri said that on the day he found out her mother was pregnant, he used all his persuasive powers to convince Karen to abort the baby—because he knew the pregnancy could split the church and ruin both their families. Initially, Karen resisted but, without the benefit of adult advice, eventually caved in to his demands. He set up the abortion appointment.

But guilt formed and slowly grew in Alan's heart until, finally, the night before Terri's life would have been sucked away, heavy conviction pressed down on Alan. The next day, rather than taking Karen in for an abortion, he talked her out of it.

Reading Alan's e-mails, Lee realized he had stopped fasting at the precise time Alan decided not to abort his child. Lee's prayer and fasting had brought on Alan's change of heart. All along Lee had known he was fasting against something Satan wanted to destroy. He thought he was fasting for unity in the church and the two families.

He was actually battling for the life of a child.

Without knowing it, Lee had obediently fasted to "the conclusion of the matter." And in doing so, he saved a life.

(JST)

"Here is the conclusion of the matter: Fear God and keep his commandments, for this is the whole duty of man." (Eccles. 12:13)

53. Childless and Angry

After Linda Rossi lost her baby in mid-pregnancy, the doctor assured her she would have no trouble getting pregnant again. He couldn't have been more wrong. Months passed with no signs of pregnancy.

Linda cried. She begged God for a baby. She questioned him. She exploded in fury at him. She tried to bribe him.

Nothing worked.

Childbearing years crawled past as Linda scribbled angry prayers and deep longings into her prayer journal, but none of it changed God's mind. Gradually, however, Linda changed. One day she journaled her surrender, *Okay, Lord, you win. I'm tired of trying to do things my way. It's like I'm swimming against your current. No more fighting, no more excuses. I want your will, not mine.*

Three weeks later, her obstetrician retired and she was forced to find a new doctor.

During her first visit, the new doctor figured out why she hadn't been able to conceive. Less than a year later, she delivered baby Nick, complete with a set of healthy lungs and a full mop of dark Italian hair. Two years after that came Ben, then Julia.

Later, Linda asked God, *Why did you make me wait? Why didn't you send me to that doctor when I first heard about him years earlier?*

"Me make you wait?" God seemed to say. "I was waiting for you to stop fighting with me."

(JST)

"God waited patiently in the days of Noah while the ark was being built." (1 Pet. 3:20)

54. Bette's Bible

I can't do it, God! Bette grasped the steering wheel with her left hand and leaned over to riffle through the glove box for a tissue. *This is my reward for all those years of praying for his salvation? He's just my pediatrician. I don't even know him that well. You want me to give him my Bible? Why can't I just go buy another Bible for him?*

She blinked to clear her vision, then turned to follow the waterfront. *I wrote the date of Eric's baptism in that Bible—and when Molly cut her first tooth.*

The voice in her heart spoke again. "He won't read just any Bible. He has other Bibles."

Why? Please, Lord. Don't make me do this. After I lost the baby, every time you comforted me with a verse, I marked it in that Bible. Every grief, every joy from those years lives in the margins of my Bible. Giving it up feels like losing the baby all over again.

Suddenly, the mighty pressure of the Lord's presence filled the car and pressed around Bette until she felt as though she couldn't breathe. She held onto the top of the steering wheel with both hands and eased her car onto the shoulder of the road. Dropping her forehead on her hands, she wept uncontrollably as wave after wave of the Lord's love and sweetness washed over her.

When it was over, she drove home, placed her Bible in a box, wrapped it in beautiful blue-striped paper and tied it with a wide ribbon. The next time she took Molly to Dr. Johanson, the emotionally cold doctor she had prayed for for years, the doctor who stiffened whenever she mentioned God, she handed him the box.

"Why, thank you." He blushed slightly and reached to open it.

"No." Bette said quickly. "Not here." She didn't know if she could endure watching him open it and reject her Bible or claim it with indifference. He had always made it clear he wanted to have nothing to do with God. "Open it later."

"Very well." He patted the top of Molly's head. "Thank you."

The door closed behind him.

Bette handed Molly her pink coat, then leaned against the examination table and pulled her daughter into a hug. "Well, sweetie, I've still got you." She cleared her throat and pressed her lips in a tight line. She could cry when they got outside. Just a little. It would help her feel better, and Molly wouldn't notice.

"I've got you too, Mommy." Molly giggled. "Let's go now."

"In a minute. We have to wait for the nurse to bring back your health card."

The door opened, and Dr. Johanson burst through. He held Bette's Bible in one hand, the box and wrappings in the other. Tears streamed down his cheeks. "I can't take this!" he said.

A lump formed in Bette's throat. He understood her sacrifice. "You have to take it." She swallowed and smiled through tears. She couldn't back out now. "And I promise, I'll never mention the Bible—or God—to you again."

And she never did.

Time passed. Her children grew into young adults who didn't need a pediatrician. She lost track of Dr. Johanson—until the weekend over ten years later when she spoke at a women's retreat in Seattle.

It was a very satisfying meeting. Bette felt as though the Lord had been there, and she had done a good job. She ended her last speech by telling the women present that they needed to be willing to do whatever the Lord asked them to do, "Even if it means giving away your Bible."

That was all.

But afterward an older woman walked up to her and asked. "Did you give your Bible to a pediatrician named Dr. Johanson?"

"Yes!" Bette searched her face in amazement. "How did you know?"

"My daughter married him. He is the sweetest, warmest, most on-fire-for-God man I've ever known. He's amazing!" the woman told her.

She didn't say he found the Lord because of Bette's Bible. But Bette is quite certain her sacrifice had a great deal to do with it.

And it was worth every tearstained page.

(JST)

"So is my word that goes out from my mouth: It will not return to me empty, but will accomplish what I desire and achieve the purpose for which I sent it." (Isa. 55:11)

"Pray the largest prayers. You cannot think a prayer so large that God in answering it, will not wish you had made it larger. Pray not for crutches, but wings."

PHILLIPS BROOKS

55. Amanda, Max, and the "Cult"

Max was frightened when his older sister accepted the Lord during her senior year in high school. When she informed him she was praying for him to "get saved," he was terrified. Just sixteen months apart, Max and Amanda had always been best friends. But now he could feel her slipping away. He determined not to lose her.

"I'm going to church with Amanda," he told his unbelieving parents.

"What? Why?"

"It's the only way to make sure she's safe. I've seen stories about cults on television. If I'm there, they can't brainwash her so easily."

For the rest of the school year, Max accompanied Amanda to services, sitting beside her in the pew like a protective knight. In the spring when the youth leader announced a summer missions trip to Mexico, Max told his sister, "I want to go."

"But why Max? It's a mission. You're not . . ."

"I don't care. It sounds fun. I want to build houses in Mexico. I'm going."

By the end of the mission trip, Max knew he wanted what his sister and the other church kids had. Result: he accepted Jesus Christ as the Lord of his life. Now brother and sister pray together for the Lord to save their parents. (JST)

"I pray that you may be active in sharing your faith, so that you will have a full understanding of every good thing we have in Christ." (Philem. 6)

56. Unworthy?

Pamela liked the twenty-minute drive to church. She used the time to prepare her heart to meet the Lord. Her husband preferred to chatter on endlessly about things that didn't matter to her. "Um-hum." She tried to follow the flow of Jeremy's conversation so she wouldn't hurt his feelings, but her thoughts kept wandering back to the Lord. *My heart feels cold this morning, Jesus. I want to feel your Spirit.*

Jeremy related the details of an article he'd read in the paper about a local runner, then without a pause, lapsed into a description of an animal show he'd watched on television the day before.

I'm sorry I was too busy to pray yesterday. Is that why you feel distant? Please forgive me, Lord. Please pour out your Spirit on me with power in the service this morning. I want to feel your presence.

By the time they pulled into the parking lot, Jeremy was describing one of the new reality shows he loved. She'd prayed for him for so long. He said he was a Christian, and she hated to judge him, but his relationship with the Lord didn't seem to go very deep. Occasionally, he even cleaned his fingernails during church. *Lord, please draw Jeremy closer to you.* How many hundreds of times had she prayed that?

Ten minutes into the service, sitting in the pew with her husband, Pamela still couldn't feel the Lord's presence. The congregation began to sing, "Here I am Lord, here I am." She meant the words of the music as she sang, but her emotions remained dead. *I know I don't deserve you, Lord, but please be merciful. Pour out your Spirit on me.*

The congregation continued to sing, "I give all myself to you. Here I am." Beside her, Jeremy's voice, somehow different than usual, caused her to glance over at him. He stood with his eyes closed, hands lifted, palms upturned, offering himself to God. God was answering her prayer of many years!

That answer to prayer called forth yet another answer as waves of gratitude poured over Pamela. God's Spirit enveloped her. All feelings of unworthiness forgotten, she wept with joy.

(JST)

"Let us draw near to God with a sincere heart in full assurance of faith, having our hearts sprinkled to cleanse us from a guilty conscience and having our bodies washed with pure water." (Heb. 10:22)

57. Fast for the Freeway

Jodi fought weakness and nausea the first day of her fast. *How will I make it through ten days of this?* she asked the Lord.

The answer came immediately, "You can't. I will do it through you. I want you to fast. Determine to do it and let me work. You want to draw close to me, don't you? You want to increase the power of your prayers, don't you?"

Jodi spent much of the second day on the couch, sick, though not particularly hungry. However, when her husband raged at her for a small offense, the temptation to comfort herself with food swept over her. But she told the Lord, *I know Tom's anger and my sickness are attacks from Satan because Satan knows my fasting releases power for you to work. Help me continue to fast.*

The third day she felt too awful to answer the phone when the prayer chain called from church. *This seems counterproductive, doesn't it?* she asked the Lord. *I'm fasting to pray and I feel too crummy to answer the phone to get prayer requests. I'm so confused I can barely think to pray. Should I stop fasting?*

"Just hang in there," the Lord seemed to say. "I fasted for forty days. You are healthy, so fasting won't harm you. I will do this for you if you simply determine to let me."

Jodi remembered reading about the great intercessor, Reese Howells, lying flat on his back in bed praying for people. Had he been sick because he was fasting? She didn't know, but she determined not to give up—even if she couldn't drag herself out of bed for the entire fast. God had promised he would do this for her, hadn't he?

By mid-afternoon on the fourth day of her fast, Jodi felt fine. Her mind cleared, enabling her to pray, though she still had to force herself to do it. She shampooed the living room carpet, ran a couple of errands, and got her haircut. Her husband gave her a big hug.

Though she felt occasional nausea, her energy continued to rise. On day six, when Tom hauled in oak flooring to lay on the cement landing to the basement, she felt good enough to help out. She praised the Lord as she pushed down to flatten the warp in the nine-year-old boards. How many times had she prayed for her husband to finish that job? She couldn't remember. She wondered if her fast had anything to do with the sudden answer to that prayer.

On day eight of the fast, her husband hitched a ride with his friend, Bill, to a football game across town. Meanwhile, Jodi did a few chores before she sat down for her evening prayer session. Just as she was finishing her prayers, she decided to pray for Tom's safety.

The prayer was brief. It didn't seem necessary to pray at length. She couldn't have explained it logically to anyone, but her prayers felt powerful. The prayers that had before seemed nothing but a dripping garden hose were suddenly transformed into a whooshing fire hose powerful enough to knock her over. All she had to do was hang on and aim.

Forty-five minutes later, Tom sank onto the couch to tell her about his ride home. "Bill stopped right in the middle of the freeway! Said he was dizzy and didn't feel safe to drive."

"Didn't he pull over on the shoulder?" Jodi asked.

"No, there was no place to pull over, so he stopped right smack in the middle of the freeway with cars whipping past. We sat there for a full two minutes before he started driving again. We're lucky we weren't killed."

"I don't think it was luck," Jodi said. She went to bed praising the Lord.

(JST)

"Is not this the kind of fasting I have chosen: to loose the chains of injustice and untie the cords of the yoke, to set the oppressed free and break every yoke?" (Isa. 58:6)

58. Something Old, Something New

Eloise pushed back from her desk and closed her eyes, massaging her temples. At age sixty-two, work seemed almost overwhelming, and she longed to quit, but she couldn't afford to. Besides, she didn't look forward to empty days at home. Thirteen years of singleness had shown her that loneliness could be worse than the stress of a job.

"Have you decided whether or not you're going to take the retirement package?" Marge asked from the next desk.

"I wish I could, but I'm going to have to pass on it. They aren't offering enough to live on."

"You look kind of down," Marge said. "Why don't you come with me to my prayer group tonight?"

Though Eloise had often declined Marge's invitation in the past, today she felt so hopeless, she accepted. At the meeting that night, Eloise felt the strong Spirit of the Lord overshadow her as the women prayed. She shared her hurts, and they targeted her specific needs with prayer. They asked God to allow her to retire, they prayed for financial security, they prayed against loneliness. After the meeting, Eloise didn't feel quite so hopeless. She could feel her faith rising as she trusted God to meet her needs.

And he did.

Shortly after that meeting, Eloise renewed an acquaintance with a widowed gentleman she had known years earlier when they belonged to the same running group. Within six weeks, they were engaged. When they needed to sell both their houses so they could marry and move in together, they prayed. Buyers were found for both houses within three days. With her husband's income added to hers, Eloise was able to accept the retirement package offered by her employer.

And Eloise is certainly not lonely.

(JST)

"Trust in the LORD with all your heart and lean not on your own understanding; in all your ways acknowledge him, and he will make your paths straight." (Prov. 3:5, 6)

59. Strange Gods In A Bag

When Theresa's French-Canadian Indian father arrived for a visit, he piled his belongings in eight-year-old Jay's room, then came into the kitchen to catch up on family news. As the conversation wound down, he said to Theresa, "Guess I'll take a walk to the store and stretch my legs." Grabbing his coat, he headed out the door.

Savoring the last of her coffee, Theresa gradually became aware of a heavy oppression settling over her. *What is this about, Lord? Why do I feel so depressed and heavy spirited today? Did my father's strange gods follow him to my house? You're my Savior, Jesus. I rejected my father's gods long ago.* Seeking God about her discouragement, she felt strongly impressed to pray a cleansing prayer over her home.

Starting in the entryway , with her open Bible in her hands, Theresa began praying aloud within each room. *God, bless those who enter here. Let no evil penetrate our home through this doorway.* Into the living room she marched, then the kitchen. *Jesus, let your presence and holiness fill each space, each person who lives here.* Theresa walked into her son's bedroom, which her father was sharing for the week. *Oh Lord, thank you for Jay. Don't let him forget your love, keep him pure, cleanse this room. . . .* Suddenly, fear engulfed Theresa. She felt the hair on the back of her neck stand up as she felt a strong force in the room.

Heart pounding, Theresa ran to the living room and fell on her hands and knees, her Bible in front of her. *Lord, what is going on?* she prayed. From deep within, faith and courage rose up, filling her spirit. *You're bigger than any problem, Father. Your Word will deliver me.*

Determined, Theresa strode back into Jay's room to face the enemy head on. She closed her eyes and spoke forcefully to the satanic powers, thrusting her right arm forward with each command. "This room belongs to the Lord. I bind all evil spirits in the name of Jesus. You have no authority here. The blood of Jesus is against you. Get out!"

Opening her eyes, Theresa discovered she was standing directly in front of a small black bag belonging to her father. In the bag were items her dad used when he worshiped his gods—an eagle's claw, a feather, and a silk cloth. More emphatic than before, her palms stretched toward the bag, Theresa spoke with authority to the satanic powers: "Greater is he who is in me than you who are in the world. I bind your power in the name and blood of Jesus."

A serene peace overwhelmed Theresa. She knew God had won the victory over any satanic power in the room. Finally relaxed, she headed for the kitchen to get dinner started.

(PP)

"If you forsake the L*ORD and serve foreign gods, he will turn and bring disaster on you and make an end of you, after he has been good to you." (Josh. 24:20)*

"He will cover you with his feathers, and under his wings you will find refuge; his faithfulness will be your shield and rampart." (Ps. 91:4)

"Pride prevents prayer, for prayer is a very humbling thing."

AN UNKNOWN CHRISTIAN,
The Kneeling Christian

60. Can't Stop Us

One atheist student complained about prayer at graduation. The ACLU filed suit.

The principal made an announcement. "There will be no prayer at graduation." No one liked it, but all agreed they were helpless against the law.

Graduation night arrived; the seniors filed in. The principal stood at the podium. "Let us pause for a moment of silence."

At first, you could hear a pin drop. Then one small voice began and four thousand others joined in. Soon the huge auditorium thundered as one, *"Our Father, who art in heaven, hallowed be thy name . . . "*

(JST)

"Do not be afraid; keep on speaking, do not be silent. For I am with you, and no one is going to attack and harm you, because I have many people in this city." (Acts 18:9, 10)

61. Is this an Artifact?

Eight-year-old Daniel dashed into the kitchen and plopped a dirt-covered chunk of gravel onto the Formica counter. "Look, Mom!" he shouted. "I found an artifact in the garden."

Jenny stopped kneading her potato bread and gazed into her son's beaming face. He had been finding "artifacts" beside the driveway and in the yard all week. "Sweetie, I'm afraid that's not an artifact." His shoulders drooped and her heart constricted.

"It's not?"

"This is important to you, isn't it?" she asked.

Tears filled his eyes. "I really want to see an artifact. Are there any around here?"

"You mean here in Bloomington?"

"Uh-huh."

"Well, Indians used to live here." Jenny washed her hands and led him into the dining room. She found the social studies book she used to home school him. Leafing through the pages, she located a picture of several lined-up arrowheads. "Indians who lived in this area made these."

"I don't want to look at a picture. I want to see a real artifact," Daniel insisted. "Can't we pray and ask God to help me find one?"

Jenny wondered at the wisdom in praying about an inanimate object, but Daniel's desire for one seemed so strong. "Um . . . I think it would be all right to pray for that." Jenny pulled her son close and closed her eyes. *"Dear Jesus, the Bible says you give us the desires of our hearts, and finding an artifact is really important to Daniel right now. So would you please help him find one? Thank you."*

Three days later, Jenny's sixteen-year-old nephew came over to take Daniel for a hike in the woods behind their home. An hour later, the boys rushed back into the house.

Daniel waved a large Indian spearhead over his head. "I found an artifact!" he shouted excitedly. "I walked on a log over the creek and jumped down and started digging in the sand and—Bam!—there it was! God helped me find an artifact!"

As he chattered on, Jenny watched his shining face with a sense of awe, amazed that God loved her son enough to answer his prayer by leading him to an Indian spearhead buried beside a creek hundreds of years earlier.

(JST)

"What is man that you are mindful of him, the son of man that you care for him?" (Ps. 8:4)

62. Caught Smuggling in Russia

Twenty-seven-year-old Nancy Riemer followed the gray-uniformed Russian guard past the long customs table piled with luggage and down a dreary hallway, dread making each step heavier than the last. She had messed up. And her stupidity could land her in a Russian prison.

Out a window to her right, snow fell on the van with an eagle painted on the side. Because it was illegal for Christian groups to tour Russia, the leader of Living Sound had disguised the van to look like a regular tourist bus. No one could possibly know it belonged to a Christian singing group, at least, not until now. Not until a customs guard found the notebook Nancy had forgotten to remove from her suitcase.

To calm herself, Nancy began silently quoting the first chapter of James, "Consider it pure joy, my brothers, whenever you face trials . . ." It had taken her all summer to memorize that chapter, but now she was grateful she had put in the effort. She needed comfort.

Though the notebook had aroused suspicions, Nancy was sure it wouldn't harm her Russian friends since she had disguised the testimonies and names of the Christians she had met and written about. However, she was in terrible trouble if the guards discovered she was smuggling letters to the outside world.

Nancy clutched her heavy coat around her and followed the guard into a small windowless room. She vaguely wondered if she shivered from cold or terror. He motioned toward a bench beside a bare table, and Nancy obediently sank onto it; her mind churning with thoughts of the letters and papers stuffed in her clothing and knee-high boots. Though the Russian Christians were protected because full names and addresses had been left off the letters, she would be in trouble if the guards found them.

The guard left the room, and two squat Russian matrons scurried in, closing the door behind them. Jabbering in Russian, they gestured for Nancy to remove her clothing.

"What?" Nancy pretended not to understand, though it was obvious they wanted to search her. "I don't know what you mean." She spoke slowly, loudly, the way people often do to foreigners who speak a different language than they do. The women continued to motion for her to strip.

Finally, in exasperation, one of them indicated for Nancy to stand up. Unable to feign ignorance any longer, Nancy slowly rose from the bench. The women patted down her sleeves . . . her sides. She breathed in through her nose, out through her mouth in an effort to remain calm. Nancy tried to form the words of a prayer in her mind, but she was so terrified she couldn't remember how to pray! "Consider it pure joy," the verses from the first chapter of James slipped into her thoughts, "whenever you face trials." The women patted the back of her coat and down her legs. Nancy waited for papers to fall onto the floor. "Perseverance must finish its work." The words kept flowing into her mind. "If any of you lacks wisdom, he should ask God." The women backed away, fists propped on hips, shaking their heads in frustration. No papers had fallen. They hadn't found a single letter!

Nancy collapsed weakly onto the bench, and a sigh of relief escaped her.

The women watched her with narrowed eyes and lips pressed into tight lines. Then a knowing look glinted in the eyes of one of the women, and her stubby finger pointed at Nancy's legs. Before Nancy could react, the other woman bent down and unzipped one of Nancy's boots. Nancy gasped. Letters and papers scattered across the concrete floor. Nancy went hot, then cold and clammy. She thought she might pass out. The two women scooped up all the papers and rushed from the room shouting excitedly and waving the letters in the air.

Nancy's teeth chattered and her knees hopped up and down—her terrified body reacting of its own volition. She tried to pray, but the only words that took shape in her mind were from James chapter one. She started quoting it again. "Consider it pure joy." But she could only get as far as verse five, "If any of you lacks wisdom he should ask of God," before her mind froze up. She tried it five times, but couldn't remember a single word past the part about wisdom. Horrified, she realized she couldn't even quote James any more.

Struggling not to cry, she bit her lip until she tasted blood. Putting on a brave appearance was her only weapon against people of this culture. Russians respected strength and pounced on weakness. She didn't dare look weak.

One last time she tried to quote James. But this time, when her mind seized up at the wisdom statement, understanding flashed through Nancy's mind. God was telling her to ask for wisdom.

In her fear, she managed to whisper a simple, one-word prayer, *Wisdom.*

God's answer was immediate . . . and strange. "Chew gum, smile, put your hands on your knees and push down."

Nancy pulled two sticks of gum from her coat pocket and crammed them into her mouth. She leaned forward and placed trembling hands on her knees, fingers turned inward, elbows out.

Five stern guards marched into the room. Nancy pushed down on her knees. Hard. They stopped in front of her and stared. She looked at the guards and smiled, chewing and cracking her gum.

For four hours, they grilled her in broken English. She chewed and smiled until her chewing gum got hard and stale and the muscles in her face felt sore. The entire time, she sensed the presence of two angels, one on either side of her, giving her strength.

Near the end of the interrogation, one of the guards brought in Nancy's personal Bible, the one he had confiscated from her suitcase. Sitting in a straight-backed chair at the table, he began to leaf through the pages, laughing and ridiculing God's Holy Word, in a thinly disguised attempt to intimidate her. It backfired. Fury rose in Nancy.

A sudden boldness surged through her. How dare he! She leapt from the bench, strode over to the table, and grabbed the Bible from his hands. Turning to the third chapter of John, she thrust it under his nose and jabbed her finger at the sixteenth verse. "Read that!" she commanded.

To her utter surprise, he did as she instructed. "For God so loved the world that he gave his only begotten Son . . ." He looked up at her, sneering. "So?"

"So God loves you!" She leaned close and actually shouted at him. "And don't you ever forget it!" She stomped back to the bench and plopped down with her arms crossed, no longer smiling. Righteous anger had dispelled all fear. They could question her all they wanted, but they'd better not make fun of Jesus in front of her!

The man at the table turned his back to her and leafed through some papers. Three of the guards, who had been watching the exchange, appeared to lose interest and chatted among themselves. The fourth approached her and bent over to place his mouth close to her ear.

"Most people in Russia do not believe in God," he whispered in a heavily accented voice, "But some do." He immediately stood and walked over to join the other guards. Only Nancy had heard him.

The guard at the table abruptly held a sheet of paper toward her. "Sign this," he said.

"What is it?"

"It is paper saying you are smuggler. If you confess, you go free."

Nancy accepted the pen and signed the paper. Ten minutes later, Nancy and her group loaded into the van with the eagle on the side and drove over the border into Finland. Safe at last.

(JST)

"But when they arrest you, do not worry about what to say or how to say it. At that time you will be given what to say, for it will not be you speaking, but the Spirit of your Father speaking through you." (Matt. 10:19, 20)

63. Escape to Freedom

Ion Sandu's fingers traced a circle around his wife's face. "If God says I should leave Romania, he will keep me safe."

"You're a fifty-seven-year-old man with fourteen children, Ion." Her dark eyes probed his. "Much younger men die crossing the border every day."

"Our son made it . . . all the way to America." Ion couldn't ignore the surge of pride.

"And we haven't seen him for three years."

A tear slipped from the pool in Maria's eyes and slid down her face. "We may never see him again."

"Our prayers kept him safe. You will pray for me, our friends will pray; and I will make it, too. Then you will join me, and we'll live with him in America."

Maria giggled, jiggling loose two more tears. "What do you think, his small apartment would hold thirteen brothers and sisters as well as the two of us?"

"You know what I mean." Ion laughed. How could she still look so beautiful after bearing him fourteen children? "We'll ask for prayer tonight."

Two hours later, Ion and Maria glanced both directions before knocking on the door of a large, white house. The door opened, and their friend Lydia ushered them in. A small group of Romanians waited in the living room on couches and chairs. It appeared Ion and Maria were the last to arrive for the forbidden prayer meeting.

"I'll keep my coat," Maria whispered when Lydia offered to take it. "It can be chilly in the spring."

Lydia nodded, and the three of them found seats as worship commenced. The group lifted their voices in prayer, praying alternately in unison and individually.

"Brother Sandu," Lydia prophesied, "the Lord has given me a picture of you crossing a great river."

"The Lord showed me the same thing!" another woman said.

"I saw you climbing a high hill and victoriously waving a flag on top," said a man. "Do you know what it means?"

"Yes, I know." Ion told the group of his plan to escape the dictatorship in Romania by swimming the mighty Dunaria River. "I asked God to confirm if that was his plan for me. I believe he has done that through all of you tonight."

The group agreed.

"But why would you go?" asked Lydia. "You have a big house, a good job. You will retire in a few years. Why take a chance of getting shot or drowning?"

"My children's future is not so bright. If I escape to America the government will eventually let them join me. They can get jobs based on merit, not bribes. They can worship God openly there."

"You risk death," Lydia said.

"Not if God wants me to go, and you all hold me up in prayer."

"We will pray, of course."

A month later on June 17, Ion and nine other men boarded a train bound for the city of Hurculane. Ion rested his head on the back of the seat and faced the window. The purple mountains of his homeland moved slowly behind the yellow-green of new leaves rushing past. He knew he would never see Romania again, but would he ever again embrace his wife and children? With an aching heart, he closed his eyes in prayer.

Three hours after their journey began, they exited the train. Each man carried a bag with a flattened inner tube and food. As darkness erased the hulking buildings of Hurculane and replaced them with pinpoints of light, the ten friends slipped into the forest bordering the train tracks. They walked until the morning sun metamorphosed the trees from black to green. Then they hid and slept. For three days, they moved at night and hid during the day. On the fourth, they saw the river that formed the border between Romania and Yugoslavia.

Hidden by foliage, Ion lay on his stomach, watching the border guards motor up and down the river. Stories of men shot by rifles or chopped to pieces by boat propellers flashed through his mind. He brushed away negative thoughts and concentrated on the river. It was narrowest here, but the current flowed strong. It might be an even greater threat than the guards. Could a fifty-seven-year-old man survive?

Just after midnight, Ion and his companions crept from their hiding places and slid the inner tubes they had inflated by mouth earlier that day into the river. The shock of cold water snatched Ion's breath away. He fought the current, buoyed up by the inner tube and the prayers of loved ones back home. Two hours after he entered the water, Ion dragged himself out of the water and fell exhausted onto the opposite bank where his companions waited. They had all made it safely across!

An engine rumbled on the river, sending Ion scrambling up the bank. If the border guards caught them now, they would be sent back to Romania, but if they could avoid the guards and turn themselves in, they might be given asylum.

Again the men trudged through a forest. Only this time, they walked on Yugoslavian soil to the city of Nagatin. There they found a police station and, despite the language barrier, threw themselves on the mercy of the authorities.

The police tossed all ten men into a nine-by-twelve room with two holes. One small hole in the room's wall let in air; a hole in the floor, smelling of urine and feces, was the place provided for them to relieve themselves.

The wait began. It would take three weeks for the police to complete background checks and decide their fate.

Would they be sent back to Romania or allowed to stay in the country?

The men prayed, barely existing on meager food brought by uniformed guards. Sometimes, one or the other would pass out because the tiny hole in the wall didn't let in enough air for so many men.

At the end of the three weeks, the door clanked open, and the men were summoned outside. "Because you are Christians and would be beaten or killed if we sent you back to Romania, you will be allowed to stay," an interpreter informed them. "We expect you to find work and support yourselves until you can immigrate to America."

Ion secured a job on a construction site. Though he had been a machinist in Romania, he praised the Lord for giving him work as a common laborer in Yugoslavia. He rented a cheap hotel room and sent the bulk of his paycheck home to support Maria and the children. But he missed them and had no idea how long it would be before he saw them again.

Seven months after he stepped onto Yugoslavian soil, Ion stepped off an airplane in Los Angeles and rushed to embrace his son who had escaped from Romania three years earlier.

Two years and four months after Ion left them, the Romanian government released Maria and the children to join him in California. Today he continually praises God who brought him through the river to a country where he can freely worship his Savior.

(JST)

"When you pass through the waters, I will be with you; and when you pass through the rivers, they will not sweep over you." (Isa. 43:2)

64. Rheumatoid Arthritis

Doctors discovered Irma's rheumatoid arthritis shortly after her birth. "It's a severe case," they told her parents. "Your daughter will be confined to a wheelchair by age forty."

A few years later, X-rays showing bent, overlapping fingers proved the accuracy of their diagnosis, though Irma didn't need medical tests to know her arthritis was progressing. The pain told her much more than doctors could. With every barometric drop, every slight change in altitude, her hands swelled, and pain shot through them.

By the time Irma married, she required morphine to control the pain caused by weather or altitude changes. Whenever it rained, she was unable to do even simple tasks, such as holding a pencil or squeezing a clothespin. Though she took great pride and pleasure in the fresh aroma of clothes dried on the line, she was often forced to use the clothes dryer rather than hanging them outside.

Fortunately, her doctor prescribed the medication willingly . . . until he retired. "You need to find a new doctor right away," he told her. However, before Irma connected with another doctor, her morphine ran out. At the same time, she was scheduled to fly with her husband to see his family. The plane trip would mean altitude changes and pain . . . without morphine. How could she do it?

She made a desperate call to a new doctor. He couldn't see her until after the trip. Panicked, she called several friends, asking them to pray. "Ask the Lord to get me through this trip," she said. They promised to pray. She and her husband prayed also, asking God to help her "just get through the trip."

And God answered.

Irma's arthritis gave her no pain during the entire visit—not even when the plane changed altitude. It was a miracle. Back home, she praised the Lord as she resumed her routine.

But with worries about the trip behind her, small frustrations seemed to dominate her life. Every time Irma would finish hanging her laundry, rain would start, and she'd have to rush out and take the clothes off the line. The third time it happened, her husband came home from work and found her crying.

"What's wrong?" Mark put his arm around her.

"You know how much I love doing laundry." She spoke through her tears. "But every time I hang out clothes, it rains, and I have to run out and grab . . ."

They both gasped at the same time as they realized God had not merely blocked her pain during the trip, but she had experienced none since then either. He had totally healed her arthritis. And he'd sent the rain to help her recognize the miracle. Irma held her hands out in front of her, rejoicing. Mark stroked her straight fingers.

"I didn't even ask him to heal me." Irma wept with joy and gratitude. "I just asked to get through the trip without pain, . . . and he healed me!"

Today, at age fifty-three, Irma's X-rays show straight fingers. But she doesn't need X-rays to convince her of God's healing power.

(JST)

"Jesus replied, 'What is impossible with men is possible with God.'" (Luke 18:27)

65. No Ifs, Ands, or Butts

Have you ever had God answer your prayer so literally that his answer exactly matched the words you prayed? That's what happened when a group of ladies prayed one Tuesday morning for their friend Bev.

For years, Bev smoked cigarettes. She tried to quit but couldn't. "I hate being unable to stop. I hate this habit," Bev complained to her prayer group. "God is convicting me that it's sin. Please pray that I'll be able to quit smoking once and for all."

Bev was a new convert, won to the Lord by her neighbor who attended the Tuesday prayer group. Bev had invited Jesus to be her Savior and Lord, and many old habits and sins had disappeared—but not the cigarette habit.

Several women gathered around her. "Of course, we'll pray. God's got answers for you, Bev. He'll help you." Laying their hands on Bev, they prayed, *Lord, take away Bev's desire for cigarettes. Don't let her even be able to get one into her mouth. Help her stop smoking. Thank you, Father. We believe you are able, amen.*

When Bev returned the following week, she had an amazing story to tell. "You'll never believe what happened after you prayed for me," she said. "When I got home, I tried to smoke a cigarette—but a wall seemed in front of my mouth. When I raised a cigarette to my lips, I couldn't push it into my mouth no matter how hard I tried. When I told my kids, they said, 'Yeah, Mom, right . . . Let's try.' But no matter how hard they pushed, they couldn't get a cigarette between my lips either! Some kind of barrier was in front of my mouth." Bev giggled. "I've quit smoking."

The prayer the women spoke the week before was this: *Don't let her even be able to get one into her mouth.* Jesus hadn't just taken away her desire; he'd put an impenetrable wall before her lips.

(PP)

"Therefore confess your sins to each other and pray for each other so that you may be healed. The prayer of a righteous man is powerful and effective." (James 5:16)

"Prayer does not need proof, it needs practice."

WILLIAM EVANS

66. Turned by Unseen Hands

Lizzie crunched through ankle-deep snow in the early Minnesota darkness. Smoke rising from chimneys and warm light shining from houses lining the street only seemed to emphasize her despair and loneliness. She dabbed at her cheeks with an embroidered handkerchief. "If I don't stop crying, my face will be as chapped as my lips," she thought.

Knowing her husband wouldn't stumble into the house until after the bars closed in the wee morning hours, she had left her four younger children at home in care of the oldest. Sunday evening services started in a few minutes, and she desperately needed to find comfort at church. She had little hope that would happen.

Where are you, God? Why doesn't church bring me peace? Lizzie paused on the corner of Hawthorne and First before turning left, toward the church she attended. *No one can help me but you. Where am I supposed to find you if not at church? Please meet me there tonight.*

Unexpectedly, two hands gripped Lizzie firmly by the shoulders, turning her in the opposite direction—to the right. "Who . . . ?" Lizzie whirled to face the owner of the hands, terrified. No one was there. What was happening?

Lizzie glanced up and down the road. Large snowflakes floated silently onto an empty street. She could still feel the invisible hands on her shoulders, pushing gently, guiding her toward the only other church within walking distance in her small town. At first, she resisted, then, as her fear subsided, she surrendered to the hands. She walked slowly at first, then faster.

When the small evangelical church came into view, she hurried toward the brightly-lit building, breathing hard with exertion and anticipation. And the instant she stepped into the warmth of the sanctuary, Lizzie knew she had found God.

That night, Lizzie heard the story of salvation for the first time in her life. Joyfully, she knelt at the altar and gave her life to the Lord. In return, he gave her the "peace that passes understanding" that she had sought for so long.

(JST)

"A man's steps are directed by the LORD. How then can anyone understand his own way?" (Prov. 20:24)

"And you also are among those who are called to belong to Jesus Christ." (Rom. 1:6)

67. Postpartum Depression

Six months after the birth of her third child, Sylvia still struggled with depression. Negative, bizarre thoughts tormented her. She wanted to dismiss it as simple postpartum depression. She'd suffered from it after her first two children. But rather than improving, her sick, fearful thoughts worsened. She could no longer adequately care for her children or love her husband.

Lord, what's wrong with me? she finally prayed desperately. *I can endure physical illness, but I can't deal with mental illness. Help me!*

A week later, her doctor prescribed an antidepressant. "We'll start you out with ten milligrams. You'll feel drowsy at first, but the symptoms will wear off. When it does, increase the dosage to twenty, wait until the drowsiness stops, then increase to fifty, and finally one hundred. After a brief time, it will stop making you sleepy," he told her. "But there is one problem with this medication."

"What?"

"I'm afraid that once you start taking it, you will have to stay on it for the rest of your life."

Sylvia hesitated. She had prayed for help. If this was God's answer, she didn't intend to reject it, even if it meant a lifetime of dependency on a little pill. "Go ahead and write out the prescription," she said.

Shortly after she began taking the antidepressant, Sylvia's mood lifted, and she was her old self again, able to love her husband and care for her children. She followed the doctor's instructions precisely. When ten milligrams stopped making her sleepy, she increased her dosage to twenty. By the time she reached one hundred milligrams, she felt great. She thanked and praised the Lord. *I'm sure this was your idea, Lord,* she prayed. *I know you often work through doctors to heal. Even though I wish I didn't have to stay on the medication, I am willing to do whatever you tell me to do. And it certainly beats mental illness.*

But then a strange thing happened. Though her attitude remained positive, the drowsiness returned. She could barely stay awake during the day. Since she couldn't care for her children when she was passed out on the couch, once again Sylvia had no choice—she reluctantly decreased her dosage to fifty milligrams. That helped for a few days, then the drowsiness returned with a vengeance. She dropped back to twenty milligrams, then ten. Finally, when the ten-milligram tablets knocked her into a stupor, she was forced to discontinue the antidepressant completely. She worried she would soon lapse back into negative thinking.

But miraculously, the depression did not return. Her attitude stayed upbeat; her thoughts cheerful. God had led Sylvia to the medication she needed to pull her out of depression; then he weaned her off the prescription as soon as it accomplished its purpose. It's been over twenty years now, and Sylvia has never had to fight severe depression again.

(JST)

"Where then is my hope? Who can see any hope for me?" (Job 17:15)

"I wait for you, O LORD; you will answer, O Lord my God." (Ps. 38:15)

68. Benched

Eleven-year-old Kenny finished setting the table, then poured a glass of milk for himself. "Growing bodies need milk," he parroted, grinning at Mom. She smiled at him over a steaming bowl of mashed potatoes. She always insisted he eat healthy food and drink milk at every meal. Closing the jug, he limped to the refrigerator and set it on a shelf.

Mom's forehead furrowed with concern. "What happened to your leg?"

"Not my leg. It's my ankle." He took the potatoes from her and set the bowl on the kitchen table.

"Did you hurt it when you slid into second base last night?"

"No, it's been bothering me for a couple of weeks." He dropped onto a chair and pulled up to the red Formica table where his dad waited to say prayers. Mom followed him to the table and sat down, too.

Immediately after the "amen," Mom probed him with more questions. "Did you injure it at baseball practice?"

"No. It just starting hurting," Kenny said.

"When?"

He shrugged. "A couple of weeks ago, I think."

"How bad does it hurt?"

"It's fine." Kenny forked a mound of corn into his mouth, answering between chews. The last thing he wanted to do was make a big deal about a dumb ankle and have Mom yank him out of baseball.

"Don't talk with your mouth full," Mom said.

Dad and Kenny laughed.

A puzzled expression flitted across Mom's face, then she smiled. "Sorry. No more questions while you eat." But she still looked worried. "Maybe you should skip baseball practice tonight."

Kenny stopped with his glass halfway to his mouth and glanced at Dad. His father understood the importance of baseball. He knew how much Kenny loved all sports.

"You'll let us know if it gets worse won't you, Kenny?" Dad asked.

"Sure."

"Well, then, I think you can keep playing," Dad said.

Dad and Kenny looked at Mom. "Oh, all right. As long as you're careful," she said.

"Thank you!" Kenny beamed at them. "I know it'll be fine."

But it wasn't fine. Over the next few weeks, the pain in his ankle increased. When it got so bad he could no longer put pressure on it to walk, his parents made a doctor's appointment for him.

The doctor palpated Kenny's ankle, then stepped back and leaned against the counter, holding on to his stethoscope, shaking his head. "It looks like a bone infection near the ankle. We're going to have to check him into Newton Memorial for a few days."

"Not the hospital!" Kenny wailed. "I can't miss baseball!"

"Don't worry, sweetie. I'll call the church." Mom said. "Within a couple of hours, everyone will be praying for God to heal you. You'll be out of the hospital in no time."

But even with the church praying fervently, "no time" turned into twenty-nine long, miserable days. The nurses plied the ankle with hot packs; doctors ordered a variety of antibiotics. Nothing worked.

"We're going to have to scrape the bone," the doctor finally told Kenny and his parents. "We're pretty sure it will remove the infection, but there's a problem." He sighed deeply. "Since the infection is at the growing end of the bone, Kenny's left leg probably won't develop normally. He will end up with one leg a good bit shorter than the other."

Thoughts of baseball and basketball flashed through Kenny's mind, and his eyes swam with tears.

Dad squeezed Kenny's shoulder. "Couldn't we give it a little while longer?"

"And pray harder?" Mom whispered.

The doctor looked down at the floor. "Even if we do nothing, the leg's potential for growth has already been compromised."

"In other words . . ." Dad spoke slowly. "You're telling us that Kenny's leg can't grow normally—no matter what course of action we take?"

"I'm afraid so."

Reluctantly, Kenny's parents signed the permission forms, and the doctor performed the surgery the following day. Soon afterward, Kenny went home in a leg cast, doomed to never play sports again . . . unless God intervened.

Kenny's little church again called out to God to completely heal Kenny's leg. "Make it grow normally, Lord," they prayed.

"Please let me play baseball again," Kenny begged.

Six weeks after his surgery, the first cast came off, and the doctor put a second cast on Kenny's leg. The church continued to pray. After another eight weeks, that cast was removed, and Kenny moved about with the help of crutches. Finally, he walked normally, but gingerly.

One year after the surgery, the doctor pronounced both Kenny's legs normal. The growth of the left leg was keeping pace with the right leg.

Today, Ken Wimbish is a radio talk-show host who stands six foot three in his stocking feet. Over the years, two normal legs allowed him to participate in a variety of sports, and he loved every minute of it. Though some people may consider the four-inch-long scar on the inside of his left ankle ugly, Ken doesn't. It is a beautiful reminder to him of the time the medical profession ran out of answers and God healed him.

(JST)

"Then will the lame leap like a deer, and the mute tongue shout for joy." (Isa. 35:6)

69. Boatworks

I was annoyed. "Why would anyone schedule a company picnic on Sunday? Don't they know some people go to church?" I asked. Don, the girls, and I changed from our Sunday go-to-meetin' clothes into jeans and proceeded to the picnic. I grumped all the way—only to find on arrival, much to my chagrin, the picnic had been on Saturday. We missed it.

Driving from the park, Don said, "As long as we're on this side of town, let's stop at Boatworks. I noticed a sharp-looking Bayliner as we drove by. Why don't we check it out?"

The twenty-one foot Bayliner was a beauty; it didn't take long to negotiate a deal. We arranged to deliver a check and finish up the paper work on Monday.

Monday I dialed Tim, the owner of Boatworks, regarding the sale details. His wife answered, "Tim's not available right now. He's at the hospital; his son's been in a terrible accident. Joe was thrown through the roof of his car and sustained head injuries. He's in a coma, not expected to live. Even if he lives, the doctor doesn't believe he'll fully recover."

"Oh, no! How terrible for all of you." As we talked, my eyes filled with tears. This was hitting too close to home. My own brother died of head injuries in an accident when he was thirteen. "May I call our church and ask the folks on the prayer chain to pray for him? I'll be praying, too."

"That will be fine," she murmured. "We'll take care of the boat business later."

Hanging up the phone, I called the church with details of the accident. Scores of people would soon be interceding. Later that evening, sitting in my recliner, an overwhelming burden for Joe engulfed me, as if he were one of my own kids. *Lord, touch Joe. He has his whole life before him. Father, you're the Great Physician; you're able to heal him.* As I waited before God, I continued to pray, *O God, help him hang on. Strengthen him; don't let him die.*

A strong impression flooded my mind, "Call Joe out of somnolence. Pray the pons area of his brain will be healed." The pons is part of the brain stem, but I hadn't thought of it for a long time, even though I'm a nurse. And "somnolence" (sleepiness) was a word I never used.

So I prayed for Joe in the name of Jesus. I prayed that he would wake up and come out of his somnolence. I prayed for his alertness, for full health, and for healing of the pons area of his brain. *Restore damaged tissue, Lord. Let no function be lost that the pons controls. Thank you, Father, for hearing me.*

"It's done. Joe is healed. I know it!" My whole being was filled with excitement. The deep burden I felt earlier was gone. I knew Joe would be okay. I looked at the clock and realized I'd been praying for over an hour. It seemed only moments.

The next morning, I called Boatworks, feeling a little hesitant. Joe's stepmother again answered the phone. I told her that I'd prayed longingly for Joe during the night and that God had given me the feeling the Joe would be fine and that everything else would be all right. "I really don't feel you need to worry anymore about Joe," I told his stepmother.

"Thank you, thank you for your prayers. It's like a miracle. He's already opened his eyes. His condition is so stable the doctors moved him from intensive care to a regular room. He isn't speaking yet, but the neurologist is amazed at his progress."

At week's end, I called again to check on Joe's progress and get reassurance that he really was healed. His stepmother answered the phone. "Joe's been discharged from the hospital. The doctors can't believe his recovery. He's completely fine, except his tongue is a little swollen from an antibiotic reaction, which makes his speech sound a little silly. The doctor is sure it should clear up in a week or so. Joe's on his way to see his dad right now."

Incredible! God's plans are certainly not our plans. We planned a picnic. He planned a drive to the east side of town. We planned to check out a boat. He planned a miracle.

(PP)

"In his heart a man plans his course, but the Lord determines his steps." (Prov. 16:9)

"People of power are without exception people of prayer. God bestows his Holy Spirit in his fullness only on people of prayer."

AN UNKNOWN CHRISTIAN,
The Kneeling Christian

70. Handy Knowledge

Though Beverly had no idea what the "gift of knowledge" was, she felt strongly impressed to pray for it. So she did. She requested it every day, several times a day. *Oh, Lord, give me the gift of knowledge.* Nothing happened for three weeks.

Then came the long-distance phone call from Jacksonville, Florida. "I have the strangest looking thing on my hand," her father told her.

Beverly froze. Though she still doesn't understand it to this day, before he went any further, she knew. "Dad, you have to go to the doctor."

"I've already been to the doctor twice. He's keeping an eye on it. You should see it." Dad laughed. "It's a raised black thing with little bubbles floating around in it between my ring finger and my middle finger."

"You have to get to a doctor immediately," she spoke firmly to her father. "Diabetics can't afford to let things like that go."

He took offense. "Beverly, you're a teacher, not a doctor. You don't know anything about medical things. The doctor's keeping an eye on it."

She changed tactics. "How did you get it, Dad?"

"I must have had a little cut on my hand when I shoveled chicken manure for the garden." She could hear the irritation in his voice. "Let's just drop it, okay?"

"Okay, Dad."

Beverly's mother took the phone. "I agree with you, honey. I took a permanent black marker and drew around the edges of it. Within two hours, that thing had grown past my mark."

"Oh, Mom," Beverly groaned, praying silently for her father's safety, "you've got to get him to the doctor!"

"The doctor's not in today. And he wouldn't see him anyway. We've already been there twice."

As soon as the conversation ended, Beverly called her younger sister who lived two doors away from her parents. "Jodi, you have to get Dad to the doctor."

"It's Saturday, Beverly."

"Then take him to emergency."

Her sister sighed. "All right. Fine." But when Beverly called to check fifteen minutes later, her dad was still home. Beverly called her sister back.

"We called Dad's doctor, and he said to wait until Monday," Jodi said.

Beverly didn't waver. "Jodi, if you don't get Dad to the doctor today, he will either lose his hand or die. I know it."

"I don't know what you expect us to do if the doctor says he's all right," Jodi said. "I called the emergency room.

They said they can't treat him, since he's already seen his own doctor."

"That doesn't sound right to me."

"It sounded wrong to me, too, but that's what they said."

As soon as they hung up, Beverly sprang into action, driven by the urgency born of certain knowledge. Praying for wisdom and help, she called a nurse friend to get the name of a diabetic specialist in her own city of Portland, Oregon. Once she had that, she called the local hospital where that doctor worked. He happened to be in and agreed to talk with her on the phone. She explained the situation to him, then scribbled notes rapidly as he talked. At the end of the conversation, he gave her the names and numbers of three diabetic specialists in Jacksonville, Florida, where her parents lived.

The first call reached one of the doctors. Alarmed at Beverly's description of her father's hand, he said, "Give me your parents' phone number, and I'll call them myself."

When she hung up the phone this time, Beverly knew she had done all she could. She fell to her knees and prayed fervently for her father's safety.

Three hours later, Jodi called from Florida. "The doctor you called phoned Mom. After talking with her, he called the hospital and told them they needed to see Dad," Jodi told her. "When we got to emergency with him, a hand specialist just happened to be there."

"Happened to be there?" Beverly knew an answer to prayer when she heard one.

"I know. Pretty amazing."

"A hand specialist? On a Saturday? I'd say that sounds miraculous!"

"The specialist said he'd never seen anything like Dad's hand. He took pictures of it for a medical journal, then cut away the black thing plus a lot of other skin. They may have to skin graft his hand."

"We'll pray they don't," Beverly said.

"Sis?" Jodi sounded like she might cry. "The doctor said if we'd waited a few more hours Dad would've died or at least lost his hand."

But he didn't, because Beverly had prayed for insight and knowledge and God had graciously granted her request.

(JST)

"To one there is given through the Spirit the message of wisdom, to another the message of knowledge by means of the same Spirit." (1 Cor. 12:8)

71. The Christian Smoker

The day Yvonne became a Christian, she stopped writing her weekly column on astrology. It didn't matter to her that several California newspapers carried it, and she was beginning to make good money doing something she loved. She dropped it cold turkey. No problem. She also changed her views on feminism.

But the cigarettes? She could not give them up, would not give them up. Wouldn't even consider it. She smoked in the bathtub. She sneaked out of church in the middle of sermons to smoke. She smoked so much it sickened her husband, who also smoked. Watching her addiction led him to throw away his cigarettes and never touched them again.

Mary, her Mexican housekeeper, wiped down Yvonne's walls, removing the brown film. "Christians shouldn't smoke," she scolded. Yvonne let her chatter on because she loved Mary so much—after all, Mary had led her to the Lord. But Mary went too far the day she told Yvonne she wouldn't be allowed to smoke when she came to her home for dinner.

"I can't get rid of the stink," Mary said.

Blind fury rose in Yvonne. The nerve of the woman, telling Yvonne not to smoke in her house! She fired Mary on the spot. She could now smoke in peace, but she was forced to admit she was an addict, held captive by nicotine.

She shot prayers up to God about the cigarettes. She prayed in the car; she prayed in the shower—which is where God finally spoke to her about her habit. "I love you right now, Yvonne," she felt him say, "even if you can't quit smoking. Just give it to me, and we'll work on your habit together. If you quit smoking today, you'd still be imperfect. We'd still have plenty to work on."

After that, Yvonne relaxed, trusting in God's love.

Several months later, a man she and her husband met at a Christian Businessmen's meeting invited them to hear him preach at a small Spanish speaking church. It happened to be Mary's church. Yvonne's heart sank. The last person she wanted to see was Mary. Nevertheless, though she dreaded the evening, she decided to go to support their friend. When she walked into the church, she scanned the crowd, looking for Mary. To her relief, she didn't see her in the audience.

Their friend's sermon touched her heart. When the service ended, Yvonne joined the long line of people waiting to be prayed for by three men on the platform.

The line barely moved as the men lifted their voices to the Lord. A yen for a cigarette poked into Yvonne's thoughts. She had gone too long without smoking. She wondered why she had decided to wait in line, or if she would be able to stay much longer. The yen grew into burning desire. She began to fidget. "This is ridiculous," she told herself. "I'm going to spend forever waiting for the men to pray for me, then I'll light up a cigarette as soon as I get out the door."

With only two people ahead of her, Yvonne glanced at the front pew. There sat Mary, listening to the prayers of the men, praying along with them. Yvonne fought the urge to bolt, but she had wasted too much time to leave now. It was nearly her turn. She stayed in line.

Finally, she stepped onto the platform and told the men she needed prayer to quit smoking. The men placed hands on her head and shoulders. They prayed that the desire for cigarettes and nicotine would leave her. She could sense Mary praying, too.

After a few more words of prayer, dry heaves racked Yvonne's body. Along with them came an inner assurance that the one "who the Son sets free is free indeed." When the prayer session ended, Yvonne hurried to the bathroom for more dry heaves.

She hasn't touched a cigarette since that day. As for Mary, though she didn't return to work for Yvonne, they have become dear friends again. If ever the urge for a cigarette comes over her, she just says, "So, if the Son sets free, you will be free indeed," and the temptation flees.

(JST)

"So if the Son sets you free, you will be free indeed." (John 8:36)

72. Fall from Larch Mountain

Lana watched her son kneel by his backpack, carefully packing the last items. No school for two days and beautiful Indian summer weather beckoned five close friends to Larch Mountain for one more camping trip before their senior year got underway. As he drove away, Lana sank down by the rocking chair and began talking to God, her recent burden for Jesse pressing heavier than usual.

Lord, I can tell something is wrong with Jesse's walk with you. Maybe it's just senioritis, but he seems so full of himself, so . . . arrogant. It's like he's doing things his own way and thinks he doesn't need you.

A picture of Jesse's growing-up years flickered before her. *He used to have such a kind, gentle spirit, Lord. I remember his fervent love for you. Bring him back to that. Make him a leader who will model those right attitudes to others.*

A leader! Where did that come from? She just wanted him to love the Lord the way he used to. She wanted him to lead people to the Lord, not be someone great. Lana glanced at her watch, 9 AM—time to get some housework done.

Throughout the day, Lana continued to pray for her son. She talked to the Lord while vacuuming and dusting; she prayed as she polished the antique oak dining table. She was still praying at 5 PM when she put the salmon in to bake. She lifted it from the oven at 5:30, and placed it on the table in front of Brian, her husband, just before the phone rang. She answered on the second ring.

"Mrs. Alexander?" asked a voice from the other end of the line.

"Yes."

"I'm afraid there's been an accident."

Lana reached out to steady herself against the counter, unable to answer. Unwilling to believe what she was hearing, she grasped only snippets, "Fell fifty feet over the cliff, then tumbled two hundred more . . . friend Travis slid down to him and cleared his airway . . . "

"Fell?" Lana murmured. Brian picked up the portable phone and walked over to stand beside her.

The voice continued, " . . . unconscious . . . rope too short for rescuers to reach them . . . rescuers still can't reach him."

"Can't reach him!" Brian's voice suddenly sounded too loud. "How long has he been down there?"

"He fell about two this afternoon."

"Three and a half hours! Is he . . . ?" Brian's words trailed off.

"He's alive, but . . . " the voice paused, "the friend with him says he's only breathing a few times a minute."

Lana gasped.

The voice said, "We need you to stay where you are so we can contact you as soon as we get him out. We're going to airlift him to Portland."

Brian hung up and sank onto a hard-backed chair. Lana stumbled toward Jesse's bedroom, leaving the phone dangling. Out of the corner of her eye, she saw Brian settle it on the hook. Would Jesse live? Was he gone already?

Sinking down by her son's bed, she lifted his Bible from his nightstand. Tears welled up, but she willed them not to flow. She must think, must pray. Thumbing through the Psalms, the forty-sixth chapter stopped her: "Therefore we will not fear, though the earth give way and the mountains fall in to the heart of the sea." The words seemed to spring to life in her heart.

Yes, Lord! That's how I feel. My world has fallen apart. Jesse has fallen off the mountain. Her eyes scanned the verses. "Be still, and know that I am God."

The words lived in her for the next hour and a half, sustaining her until the life-flight nurse called at seven to say Jesse was on his way to Emmanuel Hospital.

" . . . know that I am God." Scripture comforted her through the drive to the hospital. It held her steady as she watched paramedics unload her son's still form from the helicopter. "Be still."

I know you are God, she whispered. *You hold us in your hands.*

But she couldn't stop crying.

She cried at the sight of her beloved son lying comatose in intensive care. Would he live? She cried as visitors tried to comfort her. She cried, begging God to heal Jesse. She cried until her head throbbed, and she could no longer breathe through swollen nasal passages. She tried to be still and focus on God, but it didn't work any longer. All she could think about was her son.

Four days after the accident, in her bedroom, once again she turned to God in desperation. *Give me some word from you. You have to show me how to do this,* she told God, sobbing. Hungrily, she flipped through the Psalms and on to Isaiah, pleading with the Lord to speak help to her. She stopped at Isaiah 55.

"I will make an everlasting covenant with you," verse three said, "my faithful love promised to David."

Are you making a covenant with me, Lord? Just for today, can I put Jesse's name in that verse and take that promise for him? She read the verse again, inserting Jesse's name in the place of David's. " . . . my faithful love promised to *Jesse*. See, I have made him a witness to the peoples, a leader . . ."

A leader! That's the word she had prayed for Jesse the day of the accident. God had known what lay ahead of Jesse before it happened. He had graciously called her to prayer that morning so she would be strengthened when the inevitable happened. And now he'd keyed her in on the exact word he had prompted her to pray for Jesse that day.

He was showing her he still had plans for Jesse's life. God intended to heal her son.

Praising and thanking the Lord, Lana walked to the kitchen and rummaged through the refrigerator. The salmon she had baked four days earlier was still good. She cut off a chunk and carried it to the antique oak table. It was the first food she had eaten since the accident, and it tasted fabulous.

Three months later, Lana and Brian took Jesse home. After a long recuperation, he was once again healthy. Lana continues to pray for him to become the leader God wants him to be.

(JST)

"The LORD upholds all those who fall and lifts up all who are bowed down." (Ps. 145:14)

73. Altar-ing the Accident

4 PM Glancing at my watch as the afternoon church service ended, I rose from my seat to leave. A voice spoke to my mind. "Go forward and pray."

I have nothing I really need to pray about, Lord. And Bob has been with the children all afternoon. I should go relieve him, I argued.

Again, I sensed a strong, urgent impression, "Go forward and pray." I walked forward, doing mental inventory, wondering what I was to pray about. Nothing came readily to mind.

Moving past the crowd into the prayer room, I knelt down, and immediately an overwhelming burden filled my spirit. Sensing someone was in desperate trouble, I began to cry out to God. *Oh, Father, help whoever is in need. Keep them, protect them, and let your love and power flow to them right now.* Although I had no understanding of who I was praying for or what the specific problem was, I continued to intercede intensely for half an hour.

4:30 PM Finally, I felt a peace in my spirit and rejoined my husband and our youngest daughters.

* * *

4 PM Back home, our sixteen-year-old son, Doug, had time on his hands and a brand new driver's license burning a hole in his pocket. The Buick Regal sat in the garage. Doug and his buddy, Jim, climbed into the car, determined not to waste a perfect afternoon. Wow, freedom! Pretty sweet. Doug flipped the radio on and headed for the country road. "Fasten your seat belt, Jim," Doug said, stepping down on the accelerator.

"Seat belt? Ya gotta be kidding." Jim complained, but he buckled up.

Doug hadn't worn his belt lately either, but today it seemed a good idea. The throttle on the car had stuck yesterday when he drove uptown. But that was the last thing on his mind right now.

In minutes, the boys approached a sweeping left turn. Doug punched the gas pedal as they rounded the corner. The pedal stuck, and they swerved into the gravel on the right side of the road, barely missing some low-hanging tree limbs. Doug overcorrected the steering wheel, and they shot across the road.

Straightened out now but in the wrong lane, Doug looked up. Less than fifty feet away, closing fast, a red car sped straight at them. A woman gripped the wheel, eyes wide with terror.

Doug steered left. His tires caught the edge of the ditch, and they careened in, smashing the side of the car as it ground along. The red car whooshed past, mere inches away as the Buick shuddered to a stop in a cloud of dust.

Doug and Jim crawled out, unhurt but badly shaken. They gazed at the car. The front axle, hood, and left side of the Buick were totaled.

4:30 PM Police arrived almost immediately after the accident to help the boys and drive them home.

Later that evening, Doug called, and I understood my burden . . . and why God had spared me detailed insight as I prayed that afternoon.

(PP)

"May the Lord answer you when you are in distress; may the name of the God of Jacob protect you. May he send you help from the sanctuary." (Ps. 20:1, 2)

"What miracles of the spiritually . . . dead would God perform for us if we were prepared to go deeper and deeper in prayer for others?"

JOY DAWSON,

Intercession: Thrilling and Fulfilling

74. Running on Empty

Anchorage, Alaska, Mid-December.

"I sure hope we won't be sorry about this," said Karen Hilker, handing her husband the last suitcase. "Nobody in his right mind drives the Alcan Highway at night."

Jeff stowed the suitcase in the trunk of their little Ford Escort. "We'll be fine." Patiently, he repeated the list of precautions he'd taken. "We've packed a sleeping bag for Amy in case the car heater can't handle the drop in temperature; I've included extra antifreeze to keep the gas line from freezing; and the service-station directory is on the front seat. I used a red pen to circle the stations which stay open in the winter at night."

With deep misgivings, Karen bundled their ten-year-old daughter, Amy, into the car, and the three headed for the "lower forty-eight" and a long-awaited holiday with their families.

A fresh snowfall lent a beautiful eeriness to the silence of the black Alaskan night. Amy curled up on the backseat and fell asleep. Hours passed. Karen tried to stay awake to keep Jeff company, but she dozed off, only to awaken shivering.

She glanced toward her husband. "You doing okay, hon?"

"Hmmm," came his noncommittal reply.

As Karen pulled gloves over her icy fingers, she thought of the weather reports forecasting temperatures of 40 degrees below zero. She reached back and spread the sleeping bag over their daughter.

"Where are we?" Jeff didn't respond.

Karen turned toward her husband. She watched him repeatedly scan the horizon, then glance down at the car's lighted instrument panel."What's wrong?" she asked. Leaning sideways, she caught sight of the gas gauge. The needle pointed to empty. "Uh-oh."

With brows furrowed, Jeff said, "I can't understand it. I planned our gas stops carefully. We should have reached the Muncho Lake service station quite a while ago. How could we have missed the exit?"

Feeling guilty because she had drifted off to sleep and anxious to help, Karen picked up the directory, looking for answers. She studied the service stations highlighted in red. Then she flipped to the front page. "Jeff, this directory is a year old. Maybe the Muncho Lake station doesn't stay open at night anymore. Or maybe it closed down completely. Either way, it wasn't lit."

Jeff didn't reply. In the intervening silence, the cold facts paraded through Karen's mind and dropped like lead into her heart. The temperature was falling. Their car iced up easily. They hadn't seen one other car since they started. If they ran out of gas, the subzero temperature would quickly infiltrate their stranded vehicle. They had only one sleeping bag to offer extra warmth for the three of them.

Fear rushed into her heart and threatened to escalate to full-blown panic.

Then snatches of Psalm 121 flitted through her mind. This was the passage their family called the "traveler's psalm" and was quoted at the beginning of each major trip: "Where does my help come from? My help comes from the LORD, the Maker of heaven and earth. He will not let your foot slip—he who watches over you will not slumber. . . . The LORD will keep you from all harm—he will watch over your life; the LORD will watch over your coming and going both now and forevermore." A peace settled over Karen's entire being. She knew God would care for them.

Jeff broke the silence. "Where's the next service station?"

Karen consulted the directory. "Toad River, I guess."

"That's gotta be at least thirty miles from here—maybe forty depending on where we are." He sighed. "Guess we'll have to drive on fumes. Pray for us, honey, will you?"

Karen lifted her face toward the inky black sky. Remembering the psalm, she prayed, *Father, thank you that you help us in times of need. We need you now. Watch over us. Keep us from harm. Please let the gas last until we get to the next station. In Jesus name, amen.* When she finished, Karen felt God's presence envelope them.

As she gazed into the velvety black Alaskan night, she caught her breath. Shimmers of green and yellow swirled and streaked through the sky. "Look, Jeff!" she exclaimed. "The northern lights!"

He peered out the front window. "Reminds me of the pillar of fire God placed in front of the Israelites to lead them through the wilderness at night."

"I was thinking the same thing!" Karen's heart soared.

She couldn't be sure how long they drove on empty, but the northern lights danced before them mile after mile. After what seemed like hours, she spotted lights on the horizon, and minutes later they pulled into the Toad River Cafe.

They filled the car with gas and their stomachs with hot cocoa. And they told Amy how the Lord had watched over them.

Back in the car and once more headed south, Karen placed a hand on her husband's knee. She said softly, "Look at the sky, Jeff."

"I don't see anything," he said.

"I know. I haven't seen the northern lights since we came out of the cafe."

He smiled. "You think the Lord placed them in the sky to reassure us when we needed it?"

Karen rested her head on Jeff's shoulder. "It sounds like something our God would do."

(BM)

"The Lord will watch over your coming and going both now and forevermore." (Ps. 121:8)

75. Marathon Prayers

Lois suspected her sister's problems reached deeper than mental retardation. At age fourteen, when Elaine shoved the refrigerator into the middle of the kitchen in a fit of rage, Lois's parents became frightened and sent her to a Catholic home for the mentally retarded.

Elaine's outbursts grew worse there. She escaped from the nuns and ran into traffic; she flipped on the garbage disposal and thrust her hand into it; she wrapped a scarf around her neck in an attempt to strangle herself. Eventually, authorities sent her to a community foster home where not even the antipsychotic drugs that kept her in a stupor could completely control her suicide attempts.

During those years, Lois married, accepted the Lord, and moved from Ohio to the West Coast. Though maintaining contact with her sister became difficult, she began to pray. *How can I help Elaine, Lord?* she asked. *Is she autistic? Give me some hope. I hate to think of her spending her entire life in misery.*

The year their father turned seventy-five years old, Lois flew home for her yearly visit. Not wanting Elaine to miss the birthday celebration, Lois drove to the foster home to pick her sister up and take her to the restaurant. But before they could leave the house, forty-year-old Elaine curled into a fetal position in the middle of her bedroom floor and threw a tantrum.

Lois began to pray aloud. *Jesus, please help Elaine.*

"Stop it, Lois!" Elaine shrieked. "Don't say that name! Don't say Jesus."

At that instant, Lois knew that the thing she had suspected for years was true—dark powers were controlling her sister. She determined to pray harder; she believed prayer could release her sister.

Back home in Oregon, Lois prayed fervently for her sister, as she trained for a walking marathon. She prayed as she walked—hour after hour, day after day—praying in faith that God would help her sister, a half continent away. As she hiked through subdivisions and panted up hills, she prayed. She prayed against anger in her sister. She asked God to dispel any thoughts of suicide. She pleaded for the Lord to keep Satan away from her sister.

Shortly after Lois competed in the marathon, her mother called. "Elaine had a seizure," she said over the phone, "but her behavior has changed. She's much calmer and happier."

Thank you, Lord! Lois prayed. *Show me how to help her.* The answer came: she would ask Elaine to write out Bible verses on index cards and mail them back to her.

Over the phone, Lois asked Elaine to do that very thing: "Will you find a Bible and copy down Bible verses and mail them back to me?" Elaine hesitated. Remembering how much she loved money, Lois added, "I'll pay you a dollar for every verse you write." Elaine gingerly accepted the challenge.

Lois sent index cards, envelopes, and stamps to Elaine. A week later, the first verse, printed in painstaking letters, arrived in the mail. Lois praised the Lord, then jotted down a verse she thought might encourage Elaine. She mailed it back to her sister in Ohio, along with one dollar. That week, she prayed for the Lord to somehow use His Word to heal Elaine.

For the next few months, on a weekly basis, the postman delivered Bible verses from Elaine. And each week, Lois sent one verse and a varying amount of dollars in the return mail. Along with it, she daily prayed the scriptures into her sister's life.

Eventually, a phone call from Ohio informed Lois that her sister no longer exhibited suicidal tendencies. Miraculously, Elaine seemed content for the first time in her life.

About that time Lois's financial situation changed. "I'm not working any more. I can't afford to pay you for verses," Lois told her sister. "But since you know how to e-mail now, would you e-mail verses to me?" Elaine willingly agreed.

It's been ten years since that first verse arrived. Elaine improved so much she was allowed to work in a workshop for mentally retarded people. She handled that so well, a local business offered her a job. Elaine faithfully e-mails verses to Lois once a week.

Lois loves getting her sister's messages, but her greatest blessing came the first time Elaine spontaneously concluded an e-mail with prayer: *"jesus for josh who is having tantrums and for bob when he paints the house and for lois when she cooks. our father who art in heaven hail mary full of grace."*

The prayer didn't sound like any other Lois had ever heard, but it revealed her sister's heart. The Lord had healed Elaine by replacing her anger with His Word—and prayer.

(JST)

"Great peace have they who love your law, and nothing can make them stumble." (Ps. 119:165)

76. Sterling's Bad Heart

The family doctor discovered Sterling's deformed heart valve before the boy's fifth birthday, but in the 1930s no one knew how to fix it. "Plan on going to college," the doctor told him. "You're going to have to earn a living with your brain, not your brawn." He held the stethoscope up to Sterling ears letting him listen to the *swish* beat . . . *swish* beat . . . *swish* beat of his own heart.

Sterling accepted the diagnosis and began to pray for God to heal him.

He continued to pray though high school and college, but the heart seemed to get worse instead of better. Every doctor's visit confirmed the existence of a bad valve. Pain sapped his energy, keeping him from sleep. He grew increasingly weak.

In his senior year, things came to a head as he tried to cram for a final exam. Pain throbbed in his chest and he sank onto his bed, face to the wall. *God, I can't stand this!* he cried aloud. *Help me.* Then he heard his own voice say, "Next time I have a physical exam, my heart will be normal."

The words shocked him and he bolted upright. What had prompted him to say that? "It must have been God," he thought. There was no other explanation—Sterling now believed he would be healed by the next time he had a physical exam.

At home a few weeks later, while cutting seed potatoes, Sterling suddenly felt strong enough to hurl a feed sack full of potatoes over the house. He made an appointment with his childhood doctor.

In the office, the doctor pressed the cold stethoscope to Sterling's chest and listened. He moved it around, listening more intently. His brow furrowed. "Jump up and down fifty times," he instructed Sterling.

Sterling jumped.

The doctor pressed the instrument against Sterling's chest again. And again. And again. "Jump up and down fifty more times," the doctor said. Sterling jumped as high and fast as he could.

This time, the doctor listened only briefly, then stepped back to study Sterling's face. "Aren't you the boy that has such a bad time with your heart?"

Sterling grinned. "I am."

"Do you want to listen for yourself?"

"I do."

With the stethoscope in his ears, Sterling heard a steady beat . . . beat . . . beat. There was no doubt. God had given him a normal heart.

(JST)

"Do good, O LORD, to those who are good, to those who are upright in heart." (Ps. 125:4)

77. Flash Flood

In the wee morning hours of July 5, 1939, the Lord awakened Etta Belle Perry to pray for her daughter, Blanche. Unknown to Etta Belle, there had been a cloud burst in the Kentucky hills. Water rushed off the mountain in torrents, causing a flash flood in the narrow gorge where Blanche slept. Though Etta had no knowledge of the storm and no idea why she needed to pray, she stayed on her knees for two and a half hours, the precise length of time Blanche, a nonswimmer, struggled in the raging waters. Etta Belle stopped praying only when she felt released from her burden as light dawned over the mountains. Though sixty lives were lost that night, her daughter survived. Here is Blanche Perry Fuhrman's story in her own words:

After my junior year in college, I returned to the hills of Kentucky to do missionary work during the summer vacation. I arrived on July 4, 1939. Sixteen of us had a picnic, then, after worship, retired to our rooms in two different boarding-school dorms. I knelt by my bed. The Lord was graciously near—nearer than usual. How I loved him! I lay down, and every time I closed my eyes, I felt him. I kept thinking of the words of a song, "I felt I could love him forever." I knew he had something special for me. Little did I realize how horrible the next few hours would be. But he knew and kept blessing me.

Five of us girls slept in our dormitory that night: Mildred Drake (a teacher), Lorene Hartley, Christine Holman, Elsie Booth, and I. At three-thirty in the morning, I was awakened by a crashing of timbers and Lorene's voice calling, "Wake up, girls! Something awful is happening. We're having a flood, an earthquake, or a landslide. I don't know which!" I jumped out of bed to see the walls distorted.

We girls rushed into the hall. Lorene, looking at her watch said, "Three-thirty." Then came an awful roar, a crashing of timbers, a flickering of the gaslights, then total darkness. The building gave a lurch, and a groan. It had gone off its foundations.

I cannot describe my feelings. The water rose twenty feet in five minutes. We were utterly helpless. My first thought was that we were God's children, this was his school and his water and he could do what he wanted. Great calmness came over me, and I knew I was ready to meet God.

The building shook violently, the wind howled, pictures fell from the walls, dishes tumbled across the floor. Trunks, pianos, and chairs were lashed from one side of the hall to the other. The floor opened, and furniture began to drop through. Thunder rolled; lightning flashed; the rain poured. It was dark as a dungeon.

The water kept rising. We rushed to the attic. The stairs disappeared immediately. In less than ten minutes, we floated a mile or more. The water soon rose knee deep in the attic. The lightning flared and lingered, lighting the whole attic at times.

Elsie stood by the window weeping. The devil was there to tempt and she cried out, “If we really belong to God and he loves us, why didn’t he warn us?”

I saw she was frightened, and the devil was taking advantage. How I wanted to console her! Putting my hand on her shoulder, I said, “Elsie, we’ve trusted God to save us. Can’t you trust him now? No one will ever know how you took it, but can you prove to him that you really love him by meeting him calmly?”

She turned; the lightning flashed. I wish you could have seen her face. Heaven shined all over it. She smiled through her tears and exultingly cried, “Of course. I can trust him! I don’t know why I hadn’t thought of that before. Girls! Had you thought? In a few minutes, we will all be with Jesus.”

I’ll never forget her face.

By this time the building was too dangerous for us to remain any longer. We decided to jump. Elsie went first. I saw her swim a few feet in that awful current. Then she went down. I felt sick all over. I knew she was gone. Her body was found three days later, fifty miles away.

Christine sat in the window. I can still see her big blue eyes and face as white as snow. “Are you going?” I ventured.

“I can swim but not in that current.”

“If you’ll move back, I’ll go,” I told her. “We have only a few seconds left.”

She moved, and I jumped into that awful creek of angry, swirling, muddy water. She followed immediately. As the current carried me away, I saw her clinging to the window outside the building. Her body was found later about fifteen miles away. She is also with Jesus now.

Memories of that horrible plunge cause me to shudder yet. I could not swim, therefore expected to be in heaven soon. I asked the Lord to keep me calm and sensible so he could help me if he wanted me to live. A great peace crept over me.

I realized the current was too strong for me, and there was no use fighting it. I gave myself to the current. It sent me to the bottom. I knew the human body would float if given a chance. I held my breath, relaxed, came to the top, caught my breath, then went down again. I repeated this process for two or three miles. Sometimes I would float on my back, sometimes hang onto a bit of debris, and sometimes tread water standing up.

Scriptures and gospel songs flooded my mind. The Lord was blessing me so much I felt I had to sing or my poor soul would burst. Finally, I caught hold of some driftwood and kept my head out of the water long enough to sing the doxology. I had a camp meeting in my soul.

Again I went under but bobbed up soon and saw two girls about thirty feet away floating on part of a building. I cried, "Hello!"

Startled, they called, "Who are you and where are you?"

"I'm Blanche over here in the debris," I answered. "Who are you?"

"Lorene and Miss Drake," they shouted above the roar. "What are you on?"

"The water!" I yelled back.

"Come and join us!"

"No, thanks. I'll stay here," I answered. I couldn't swim, you see.

Soon the overloaded stream plunged into the North Fork of the Kentucky River. I felt myself being dashed first against a train trestle, then against the opposite river bank, then flopped back to the center of the river again.

I held my breath as long as I could and was trying to push my head up through the debris to get a breath, when I was suddenly knocked downward to the bottom of the river. It seemed that tons of debris piled on me. I began to struggle but soon felt there was no use to fight as I would drown anyway. I wanted to get it over as soon as possible; therefore, I willingly sucked in all the water I could.

I will not try to describe the physical agony of the next few seconds. I thought. "Surely now, in only a second I will go sweeping through the gates of glory." I wondered if the other girls were drowning. I began to get anxious to see Jesus.

Suddenly, all thoughts of heaven fled. I thought of Paul's shipwreck and how some swam, others floated on boards. Then I thought of how God had called me to his service. I prayed, *Lord, if you want me to live, I'm willing. But if you are through with me, I'd like to go now, I'm so near.* He flooded my mind with promises, assuring me I would live.

I said, *You'll have to help me then. I can't float any more, I'm too full of water.*

In my agony, I had gripped a log, hoping to ease the pain in my chest. I held on to it and gradually came to the top. I felt the air upon my face, but to my horror, I could only gasp. I said, *Lord, it's up to you. Prompt me what I ought to do.*

At that instant, several other logs bumped against me. I climbed up on them and bent over, and water came pouring out of my mouth and nose. When the air struck my lungs, it felt like coals of fire.

I finally managed to get onto a small piece of a building. (There were several houses and barns in that stream.) When I was settled again, I heard voices. Lorene and Miss Drake's float had broken in two, and they were several feet apart now. I had not seen them for two or three miles, but now I bobbed up between them.

They were surprised, and Lorene called, "Where did you come from?"

"Where do you suppose?" I retorted. We all laughed and were glad to see each other.

Shortly afterwards, Lorene washed ashore. Miss Drake and I continued on downstream. I took advantage of my ride to relax completely so as to gain enough strength to sing. But I was too weak, so I sailed on. Miss Drake was rescued half a mile further.

My ten-mile journey came to an end when I picked up a two-by-four and pushed away the debris—trunks, mattresses, chairs, and boards to clear the way for my float to drift to the shore bank. I caught hold of a willow limb, threw myself into the tree, slid down to the bottom where the water came up to my neck, then pulled myself to the bank.

Daylight was just dawning over the mountains. Rain continued to pour. A snake wriggled out of the weeds and slid into the water. When I tried to walk, my hair, heavy with debris, kept pulling me over. I sat down, and for a moment couldn't remember where I was. My head was in a whirl.

Finally, pulling myself together, I followed a path that led to a mountain home. The mother and several children stared at me in horror as I explained, as best I could, what had happened.

Then she ventured, "Ain't ye scared to death?"

I said, "No. I'm a Christian, and I was ready to go."

She gave me some dry clothes, and I walked barefoot two miles across a hill where rescuers met me.

(BPF)

"You are the God who performs miracles; you display your power among the peoples. . . . Your path led through the sea, your way through the mighty waters, though your footprints were not seen." (Ps. 77:14,19)

78. Miracle Boy

On July 4, 1995, Rose Tetrick's son Michael was just an ordinary fourteen-year-old boy pushing his little sister on an air mattress in the crowded pool of a family friend.

Beside the water, Rose reclined in a lawn chair, pride and gratitude filling her as she watched her children. Suddenly, somewhere between the kiddy pool and the deep end, she saw Michael grab his head and start crying.

Michael rarely cried and never in front of people.

"Bob! Get Michael out of the pool!" she shouted to her husband over the noise of the Independence Day crowd.

Moments later, Rose settled Michael in a poolside lounge chair and handed him two aspirin and a glass of water.

Five minutes later, Michael vomited.

"He must have the flu," said Eva, their hostess. "Maybe you need to get him out of the sun. Why don't you take him in the house and let him sleep in one of the back bedrooms?"

"Thanks," Rose said. She walked into the house with Michael and settled him on a twin bed. "I'll come get you in time for fireworks," she promised. She stayed until he closed his eyes and drifted off to sleep. "Poor kid. He looks terrible," she thought.

Back by the pool, Rose shook off her concern and chatted with friends. She convinced herself that Michael just had the flu. He'd be fine.

Later, as everyone arranged chairs to view fireworks, Rose tiptoed into the house to wake Michael. He would hate to miss the fun.

What she found terrified her. Michael was stretched crosswise on the narrow bed . . . in full seizure, jerking stiffly. His eyes rolled back in his head; foam collected in the corners of his mouth.

"Bob!" Rose screamed, then grabbed the phone and called 911.

Friends dashed into the house and swarmed around Michael. By the time the ambulance arrived, the seizure had passed, and Michael walked unassisted around the bedroom.

"We can't take him in the ambulance, Mrs. Tetrick," the paramedics told Rose. "He looks fine."

But he didn't look fine to Rose. His face looked as gray as the cement around the pool, and he still complained of a headache. "He's never had a seizure before," Rose said. Something inside her warned of danger for her son.

"But he's walking on his own."

Rose summoned all her strength and clipped her words. "You will drive my son to the hospital in your ambulance."

"But . . ."

"You *will!*"

Shaking their heads, the paramedics loaded Michael into the ambulance and drove off slowly, not even bothering to turn on their flashing lights. Rose quickly dialed the prayer chain and asked them to pray for Michael. Then she and Bob piled into the car and sped to the hospital, beating the ambulance to the emergency-room door.

Within moments, Rose heard a siren and watched an ambulance with flashing lights screech to a halt in front of the emergency room. Several women and men in hospital garb pushed past Rose and Bob to converge around an unconscious Michael, frantically working on him as paramedics wheeled him into the hospital.

"He had another seizure." Rose heard one paramedic say to the attending physician. "I thought we'd lost him."

The next few minutes passed in slow motion. An IV dripped into Michael's arm. Hospital personnel closed the curtain around Michael's cubicle, shutting out Rose and Bob. A strange man in street clothes paced the corridor, occasionally peering into Michael's examination room. Finally, the ER doctor appeared in the hallway and spoke the fateful words, "Cerebral aneurysm. We're prepping Michael for surgery."

Trembling, Rose signed the surgical consent papers.

"We're in luck tonight," the doctor told them. He pointed to the man from the corridor who now wore hospital green. "He's the city's best neurosurgeon. He just happened to drop in here on his day off."

Rose looked at the clock that read midnight. She knew many of the prayer chain members would still be awake, praying. "It's not a coincidence he showed up here tonight," she told the doctor.

Hours later the neurosurgeon appeared in the waiting room, looking exhausted. "We had to cut a huge chunk out of your son's skull," he said. "And when we did, a blood clot the size of a racquetball shot out." He looked at the floor, avoiding eye contact. "I don't expect Michael to survive this. But if he does, he'll be little more than a vegetable."

For a while, panic closed around Rose, but then she squared her shoulders and walked to the pay phone in the waiting room to call the prayer chain again. She refused to accept the diagnosis. God could heal Michael if he chose to.

Over the next few days, groups from the church took turns keeping a vigil in the hospital. Praying. Supporting Rose and Bob.

God heard and answered those prayers. Within the week, Michael could walk and talk—something the doctors had said he would never do again. Soon it became clear he had all his mental capacities.

Today, Michael is a bright college student. For anyone who listens, he offers proof of his story by showing the half moon, racquetball-sized scar just above his right ear. He claims James 5:15 as his verse.

Doctors and nurses from the hospital and every prayer chain member still refer to Michael as the Miracle Boy.

(JST)

"And their prayer offered in faith will heal the sick, and the Lord will make them well." (James 5:15 NLT)

79. Starr Pray-er

Laurel Starr sensed something wrong the instant she heard her mother's voice long distance. "What is it?" Laurel leaned against her college dorm desk, cradling the phone, dreading the answer. "What's wrong?"

"I never could fool you," her mother said with a little laugh, then hesitated before answering. "I found a lump in my armpit."

"No! It's not possible! You've been cancer-free for seven years. It can't come back."

"I'm sorry, honey. The doctor says breast cancer is like that sometimes."

"I'll pray." Laurel felt as though she had to force out the whispered words.

"I knew you would. That's why I'm calling."

Gripping the handset, Laurel ran her fingers upward through her bangs, stopping to rest her hand on top of her head. "When do you see the doctor?"

"Day after tomorrow at three in the afternoon. They're going to do an ultrasound and then biopsy it."

"I wish I could be there."

"Just pray, sweetheart," her mom said. "That'll be even better."

"I will."

As soon as she hung up the phone, sobs wrenched Laurel's body. *Oh, Lord, help my mother. Please don't let that lump mean the cancer is back.* She was glad her roommate wouldn't return until evening; it would give her a chance to pray in private. She fought back fear. *Help me not to be afraid,* she pled with God.

Remembering a prayer technique she had recently learned in her college Spiritual Formation class, Laurel knelt at her bed and visualized the lump under her mother's arm. Then she pictured God taking control of the lump, dissolving it. She kept her mind focused on God, "watching" him take away her mother's cancer. The peace that passes understanding swept over her.

For the rest of that evening and the next two days, whenever Laurel thought of her mother, she visualized the lump and God dissolving it.

Shortly after three on the afternoon of her mother's appointment, Laurel returned to her dorm room to change clothes. The phone rang.

"It's gone!" her mother shouted excitedly from the other end of the line. "It's gone!"

"What? Where are you?"

"I'm in the doctor's office. He let me use his phone. I told them I had to call you. The lump is gone!" She laughed. "I'm still dressed in a hospital gown."

Laurel tried to sort through her mother's words. "How do you know for sure it's gone?"

Her mother's voice slowed and took on the patient tone she had used when she explained concepts to Laurel as a child. "When the ultrasound technician tried to locate the lump, she couldn't find it. I got so excited I grabbed the wand from her hand and probed for it myself." Her mother began talking faster. "I couldn't find it either. So I searched with my hand where it was this morning, and it was gone! I knew you'd be praying nonstop, so I had to call you!"

"You're shouting again," Laurel said with a giggle. "I prayed, but I would never have believed this. God is amazing! Prayer is incredible!"

"I told everyone in the office you're my Starr pray-er," her mother told her.

(JST)

"And I will do whatever you ask in my name, so that the Son may bring glory to the Father." (John 14:13)

80. Bibles and the Secret Police

Clive Calver of *World Relief*, an organization based in Baltimore, Maryland, shares a miraculous story from a Middle Eastern country that must remain anonymous.

A bishop helped two believers load Bibles into their car, instructing them to deliver the precious cargo to a remote village. But he did not tell them exactly where to find the town. The men left in the early morning hours, hoping to avoid detection by the secret police scattered throughout the countryside.

After driving for a while, they came to a junction in the road. Which way should they go? The steering wheel jammed, and they had no option but to turn right. So they did. Soon they came to a man standing alone on a corner. Was he the secret police or simply someone who might know the location of the village they needed to find?

Though fearful, the believers stopped, rolled down the car window, and asked directions to the village.

The man on the corner said, "You have Bibles."

Fear gripped the men in the car. "No!" they said. "Please tell us how to get to the village."

The man on the corner insisted, "You have Bibles."

Again the believers in the car denied having Bibles and started to roll up the window.

The man on the corner said, "I prayed for Bibles. God told me if I would stand on this corner at five-thirty in the morning, someone would bring me Bibles. I have my life savings. I know you have Bibles."

He handed the two believers sixty dollars. They gave him one hundred Bibles.

(JST)

248 *"Your word, O LORD, is eternal; it stands firm in the heavens." (Ps. 119:89)*

Contact World Relief at: www.worldrelief.org

81. A Grapefruit-Sized Tumor

Robert leaned over the gurney and placed his hands on the swelling in his wife's abdomen. He could feel the grapefruit-sized tumor beneath his palms. "I'm going to pray for you one last time before they take you into surgery," he whispered.

"Mmmm . . . okay." She smiled weakly and closed her eyes, already sinking into a drug-induced sleep.

Lord, remove my darling's tumor. Dissolve it right now in the name of Jesus. Feeling heat and movement beneath his fingers, Robert prayed fervently, confidently. *I know you are healing her. Thank you, Jesus.*

The attendant wheeled her into the operating room.

Minutes later, the doctor emerged from surgery shaking his head in disbelief. "I don't understand it. When I opened up your wife, I found no sign of a tumor—even though tests clearly showed it there earlier," he told Robert. "I reprimanded my staff because I thought they brought me the wrong patient."

"I prayed for her right before surgery," Robert told him. "But she was already sedated, and I didn't think I could stop the procedure. I'm confident that God healed her."

The doctor stared at him in bemusement. "Maybe you're right. It's certainly the strangest thing I've ever seen."

(JST)

"When Jesus saw her, he called her forward and said to her, 'Woman, you are set free from your infirmity.' Then he put his hands on her, and immediately she straightened up and praised God." (Luke 13:12, 13)

82. The Battle Belongs to the Choir

An answer to prayer from the Bible

King Jehoshaphat nodded at the messengers. "Speak."

News poured from them in the breathless tones of runners. "A vast army marches against you from beyond the Dead Sea." Sweat dripped from brows and formed dark splotches on tunics. "They're nearly here! They're already at the waters of En Gedi. They'll rest for a while, then attack."

Fear weakened Jehoshaphat's knees. Falling on his face in the Lord's presence, he groaned. *God, help me! I'm the king. Everyone expects me to know how to handle this, but I don't know what to do. Our army is tiny—helpless against the armies of Edom. Give me wisdom! Guide me!*

After time with the Lord, peace enveloped him, and a confident Jehoshaphat rose to his feet and summoned runners. "Quickly! Tell everyone from Judah to fast and join us in Jerusalem. We need to seek the Lord."

When the people arrived, the king stood before them in the new courtyard of the temple, praying for the Lord's help. All the men stood before the king with their wives and children. With one voice, they beseeched the Lord.

They had been praying for quite a while when the Spirit of the Lord fell on a man named Jehaziel. "Listen!" he shouted. "The Lord says not to be afraid! We've prayed; he's answered. The battle belongs to him, not us. We won't even have to fight. All we have to do is trust him, then march out, take our positions, and stand still to watch the Lord's victory."

Everyone believed the prophecy. They fell to their faces worshiping God. Afterwards, to finish off the evening, the Levites jumped up and praised the Lord with one long, ear-splitting shout.

Early the next morning, the king led the army out into the wilderness, urging them, "Have faith in God and his prophets, and you will be successful. God says we won't even have to fight." And then, just to prove how strongly he believed in God's power, he told the singers to walk ahead of the army.

"Sing!" he told them. "Praise!" And they did—joyfully.

The moment the choir began to sing and give praise, the Lord confused the enemy, and they started fighting among themselves. When the army of Judah arrived at the lookout point, there were only dead bodies as far as the eye could see. Not one single enemy soldier was left to fight. God had miraculously answered their prayer for protection.

(JST)

"As they began to sing and praise, the LORD set ambushes against the men of Ammon and Moab and Mount Seir who were invading Judah, and they were defeated." (2 Chron. 20:22)

83. Lowell's Stroke

Sylvia dialed 911 the moment Lowell's seizure hit. The ambulance arrived within minutes. Kaiser's emergency room personnel hurried him upstairs for an MRI immediately.

Things slowed after that. Sylvia called her priest, then paced the carpeted floor, waiting to hear her husband's prognosis. It was a stroke, the doctors thought, but how massive? Would he live?

Half an hour after she called her pastor, he arrived and led her to a gray vinyl chair in the waiting room so they could pray. They were in the middle of prayer when the doctor called her name.

"Sylvia?"

She opened her eyes and stood to meet him. "Yes."

"The MRI shows massive bleeding in the left rear quadrant of your husband's brain. We're going in to see what we can do, but I'm afraid we won't be able to save him."

Sylvia collapsed trembling onto her chair. Her pastor found a phone to notify his prayer network about Lowell, then returned to comfort her. Throughout the surgery, they prayed for a miracle. And they got it.

"I'm mystified," the doctor told her after surgery. "There was absolutely no sign of bleeding when we got into your husband's brain. Just a few small bleeders—which I undoubtedly caused going in. Your husband will be fine."

(JST)

"For you, O LORD, have delivered my soul from death, my eyes from tears, my feet from stumbling, that I may walk before the LORD in the land of the living." (Ps. 116:8–10)

84. Hail to the Melon

The idling of an engine on the black-top road separating the St. John's five-acre muskmelon patch from the neighbor's drew young Keith's attention. "Hey, St. John," a voice called from the car.

Keith turned to wave at Joe Lemmon, framed in the driver's window of his father's shiny new 1941 Ford. "Hey, Joe!"

"The radio says there's a big storm comin' in."

Pulling a freshly ironed handkerchief from his pocket, Keith wiped the sweat from his forehead. Out of the corner of his eye, he saw his mother drag a hoe sideways through the top of a row, blocking the plants into rectangles. She'd been up since four ironing for neighbors. Now she worked in the field, doing the job her husband had done until three weeks earlier. On the far side of the field, where their melons bordered Pettibone Lake, his two younger brothers bent over, weeding the plants. Everyone had to pitch in since Dad died.

Joe revved his engine. "Thanks for the warning, Joe!" Keith said.

Joe Lemmon nodded, and the Ford roared off down the road. Keith squinted into the hot, blue Michigan sky and dabbed at his forehead again. "A storm? Not very likely," he mused. But within five minutes, as though called forth in response to Joe's words, the temperature plummeted, and the sky darkened with swirling clouds. Wind whipped froth onto the tops of waves in Pettibone Lake.

Her skirt billowing around her, Keith's mother ran toward him, motioning for the two younger boys to join them. "We've got to pray!" she shouted above the wind. By the time the younger boys reached them, her eyes were closed, and she prayed desperately to the Lord. *Oh, God, without this melon crop, we won't have money for food this winter.*

Every couple of minutes, a "whoosh!" from the blacktop behind them told of passing cars. Keith turned his back to the road, embarrassed. He knew they needed to pray but not in public like this.

At the sound of a low rumble from the opposite side of the road, he glanced up. A curtain of hail slowly swept toward them across Clayton's melon field. Mother must have seen it, too, because her praying increased in volume. *Lord! You promised to take care of orphans and widows! Help us!* She opened her eyes and urged her sons, "Boys, pray! God will save us." Then she lifted loud cries to the Lord again.

Marble-sized hail pounded onto the blacktop and bounced along the edge of the melon patch. Desperation erased his embarrassment. Keith fervently joined his family in prayer.

For twenty minutes, huddled among the melon plants, arms around one another and shivering with cold, the family begged God for help. As they prayed, the storm circled the field, ripping through Clayton's melons on the north, wiping out the Phillips' potatoes to the east, making shambles of Sargent's corn on the south side of their field. And to the west of them, it riddled the Lemmon's corn.

Though the storm destroyed all the crops surrounding them that day, God spared their melons. A mere smattering of hail touched the St. John field.

(JST)

"Throughout Egypt hail struck everything in the fields—both men and animals; it beat down everything growing in the fields and stripped every tree. The only place it did not hail was the land of Goshen, where the Israelites were." (Exod. 9:25, 26)

85. Journey to the Edge

Anna forced herself to breathe slowly until the clutch of fear in her chest released. In . . . out . . . in . . . out . . . She glanced toward her husband, Eldon, for reassurance. His face wore a mask of concentration as he expertly navigated their car down the winding, dirt-and-gravel road. They'd left the mountain town of Stonewall, Colorado, hours ago, hours of anxiety for Anna.

She deliberately avoided looking at the breathtaking scenery outside her window—breathtaking because the ground next to her fell hundreds of feet to the Purgatory River. No bushy slope or bank of trees broke the sheer drop to the water below. They were driving on the edge of a man-made cliff, and the road had no guardrail to protect them from plunging over it.

Rounding curve after curve, Anna countered her fear with Bible verses she'd memorized: "Do not fear, for I am with you; do not be dismayed, for I am your God." *I believe you, Lord,* she prayed and deliberately relaxed her clenched hands. "Surely God is my salvation; I will trust and not be afraid."

Bang! The car lurched. Anna's heart flew to her throat. Eldon gripped the steering wheel, pumping the brakes. "We blew a tire."

The car swerved, and Anna grabbed for the armrest. They wove down the mountain road, careening from one lane to the other. Eldon fought desperately to keep the car under control.

Heart pounding and feet braced against the floorboard, Anna shot prayers heavenward, praying for their safety, thanking God there weren't any other cars to crash into. Then they hit loose gravel. The car skidded toward the precipice.

Anna leaned forward and cried out, *Lord, don't let it happen!*

The car stopped—at the very edge of the cliff. If Anna opened her door, she would step into thin air. She sank back into the seat, light-headed with relief. *Thank you, Lord! We're safe!*

"Not yet," her white-faced husband replied in a strained voice. He opened his door. "The ground under us could crumble at any moment. We have to get out."

Anna cautiously slid across the seat to the driver's side and climbed out after her husband. Weak-kneed, she joined Eldon on the road and stared at the car. "What now?"

He ran a hand through his hair. "I need to move the car away from the edge so I can change the tire. But with the flat, we can't push it by ourselves." He glanced at the road and its snake-like curves. "If we did manage to move it, a car could come around the bend and hit us."

The thought chilled Anna, even in the late afternoon heat. Yet she wondered at its likelihood. In the eight hours since they'd left Stonewall, they hadn't seen one other vehicle. "A mixed blessing," she thought wryly.

Eldon pulled the spare tire from the car's trunk, then rummaged around for the jack. Silently, she prayed, *Dear Lord, we're in a mess. You know we need help. Please send it.*

Heat radiated up from the road. Feeling the perspiration trickle down her neck, Anna wished they'd brought a thermos of water or iced tea. Eldon walked back and forth, considering the car from different angles.

"I could go for help," thought Anna, and immediately realized how senseless that effort would be. They were miles from any sign of human habitation.

The sun moved lower in the sky. Leaning against the rock cliff chiseled from the mountain, Anna found herself wondering how cold it could get up here at night. *Lord, please protect and deliver us.*

She heard the noise of the motor first. Then a road maintenance truck appeared around the bend. "Need help?" called one of the men in the truck.

Anna smiled with relief. *Thank you, Lord.*

While Eldon and the men moved the car and changed the tire, Anna poured out her heart to God. *Lord, you are so good! You saved us from death. And you're taking care of us now. Thank you. Thank you.*

The workmen returned to their truck with hearty goodbyes. Leaning out the window, the driver said, "Lucky we come along when we did. We was headin' home for dinner. Not likely anyone else'd be along 'til mornin'."

But Anna knew it wasn't luck. God had answered her prayers.

(BM)

"Be strong and courageous. Do not be terrified; do not be discouraged, for the L*ORD your God will be with you wherever you go." (Josh. 1:9)*

86. Instant Deliverance

Trisha told me about her journey through a drug rehabilitation program. After several weeks and many counseling sessions, she still felt overwhelmed by her need for cocaine. Addiction gripped her like a vise, and she felt she would never break free.

One afternoon, feeling completely defeated, she stumbled to her room where she could be alone.

She sank to her knees beside the bed. Quaking with sobs, she cried desperately to the Lord—*Oh, God, I can't do this! Wipe away my addiction!"* She glanced up at the mirror and saw an actual hand sweep across her back.

She felt instant release. The addiction to cocaine never returned.

Did Trisha have a relationship with God? I don't think so. But she cried out to him from a place of desperate need, and he heard and answered her prayer. Several years later, while on the phone with me, she accepted the Lord as her Savior.

(JST)

"The Sovereign Lord will wipe away the tears from all faces; he will remove the disgrace of his people from all the earth." (Isa. 25:8)

87. Blind Times Two

"Your vision is very bad," the doctor told Irene bluntly. "You have to stop driving."

"But I have to drive. My husband is blind because of diabetes. We won't even be able to go to church if I don't . . ." her voice trailed off.

The doctor shook his head. "The laser surgery reattached your left retina, but no one can fix the two holes in your right retina. You will eventually lose sight in that eye. There's no point in trying to remove the cataract."

Irene left the office too upset to share her problem with anyone. What would she and Jack do if she couldn't drive? By prayer meeting that evening, she still hadn't talked to anyone. She sat alone in her pew, pleading with the Lord for help.

After the service ended, a friend placed a gentle hand on Irene's shoulder. "I'm not sure why," she said, "but I feel I need to pray for you and pray for your eyes. May I?"

Irene gratefully accepted the offer, then explained her problem to the friend. The woman prayed for Irene, praying specifically for her eyes to be healed.

Two weeks later, the eye doctor pronounced the holes in Irene's retina completely healed. "I don't know how it happened," he said, "but now I can remove the cataract. You will be able to drive safely."

Irene left his office praising the Lord.

(JST)

"Then he touched their eyes and said, 'According to your faith will it be done to you'; and their sight was restored." Matt. 9:29, 30)

88. A Wayward Answer to Prayer

Twelve years ago, I began to feel the Lord push me in the direction of writing. Instead of joyful obedience, I responded with weak rationalization. *Look Lord,* I said, *you've got tons of great writers out there. You don't need me.* In spite of my objections, the urge wouldn't go away. Though I never heard an audible voice, I felt certain the Lord wanted me to write.

I tried to ignore it. But people kept bringing the idea back to me, as if they'd thought of it themselves. "You should be a writer," they'd say. I rarely replied. I had no idea what it took to become a writer, but I knew writers. I knew that the competition was stiff. Honestly, I hated the idea of having other people evaluate my work. I didn't think I could handle a single letter of rejection. No. Not for me.

Eventually, my resistance worn down, I gave in, but in a Gideon-like way. *Okay Lord,* I challenged him, *if this is you talking to me, I want you to confirm it. I don't want to waste my time working at something if it isn't you. So, here is what I'll do. I'll enter this writing contest. And if you want me to write, just let me win the contest. Then, I'll know it's your will. Okay?*

I polished my short essay and sent it to a magazine contest, confident that I would soon hear from the contest administrators. One month passed, then two. No response. I began to worry—but only a little. After all, I reasoned. I was obeying God. Surely he would take care of the contest.

Eventually, unable to wait any longer, I called the magazine sponsoring the contest. "Oh no," the lady said. "We don't notify anyone but the winners. If you haven't heard from us, you didn't win." They didn't even keep the entries. My essay lay in a New York garbage can.

Devastated, I went away with my family to a Christian family camp for our summer vacation. Had I made it all up? Did God really speak to me? What had gone wrong? I would have prayed about it, but I was too angry with God for what seemed to be a heavenly joke.

That week at camp, Dr. David Jeremiah spoke on the book of Joshua. And in the middle of the week, he covered Caleb. He pointed out that though Caleb was as qualified as Joshua (he too had given a good report after spying out the land) Caleb was rejected as the replacement for Moses. The job went to Joshua. "Imagine his disappointment," our speaker said, "to have to go home and tell his wife, 'Well, they gave the promotion to Joshua.'"

After the wandering in the desert, the Jews finally conquered the land of Canaan. In his request for land, Caleb explained to Joshua that he was as strong at eighty-five as he was forty-five years ago. Dr. Jeremiah expounded the original Hebrew. Caleb is strong because with the Lord's help, he had "kept" himself strong.

"So," our speaker concluded, "Perhaps you are waiting as Caleb did, for your moment. Are you keeping yourself strong? Are you practicing that musical instrument? Are you polishing your skill? Are you studying?"

I had to admit that I wasn't. I wanted to write—but I didn't want to work at it. I wanted the glory without the sweat. In those few moments at the end of chapel, I found myself humbled, and I rededicated my writing skills to the one who made me. Determined to try again, I promised the Lord to work at writing and leave the publishing to him.

Fifteen minutes later, I ran into the camp director outside the chapel. "What happened to that book the conference center is writing?" I asked.

"Funny you should ask," she answered. "All the notes, all the work, everything just landed back on my desk this week. The man who was going to write it decided that he couldn't. I don't know how we'll get ever get it written."

By the time I left that week, I had my first writing assignment. I would author the biography of the Conference Center's founder, Evangeline McNeill. With four children under eight, it took me six years to do the research and write the book. But when I'd finished, I worked with a professional editor who sat down beside me to explain every single red mark on every single page. "I want to teach you," she said, "because you have so much potential as a writer."

What began as pride peppered with devastation, ended with a newfound humility and the free tutoring of a genuine professional. In the beginning, I asked the Lord for his confirmation of my calling. Though his answer seemed like a clear and simple *no*, it turned out to be a more wonderful *yes* than I could ever have dreamed.

In a wayward answer to prayer, I experienced great growth.

(BN)

"And whatever you do, whether in word or deed, do it all in the name of the Lord Jesus, giving thanks to God the Father through him." (Col. 3:17)

89. Ezra's Deliverance

(A retelling of Ezra 8)

God offered Ezra, a captive priest living in Babylon, the opportunity to witness to a king. And Ezra grabbed it. He told the king, "God protects all those who worship him."

The king raised his eyebrows, impressed, then gave Ezra 7,500 pounds of gold and twenty-four tons of silver and sent him off to fix up God's temple in Jerusalem. But the one thing the king did *not* give Ezra (because of all Ezra's bragging about God) was an armed guard. It never even entered the king's mind that Ezra would need an army. The king believed Ezra's press—God would protect him.

Ezra shook with fear. Perspiration beaded on his forehead. Sure, God could protect him, but . . . he needed the king's army to escort him. Lawlessness reigned in the countryside. Bandits roamed the highways. His enemies might ambush him. He could get killed, for goodness sake!

He had to force himself not to rush back to the king and beg for an armed escort. And he didn't.

Finally, ashamed to ask the king for help after all his boasting, Ezra came up with a radical plan. Instead of asking the king for protection, he would ask God. He camped by a canal with his friends and followers, and they fasted and earnestly prayed. We don't know how long they prayed, but it sounds like they prayed harder and longer and with more urgency than ever before. Who could blame them? And . . .

God protected them. They arrived in Jerusalem without losing one ounce of silver or one life.

That's how our God is. If he says he'll do something, he does it. And he says he'll answer prayer. I wonder what would happen if we would all fast and earnestly pray?

(JST)

"I gave orders for all of us to fast and humble ourselves before our God. . . . So we fasted and earnestly prayed that out God would take care of us, and he heard our prayer." (Ezra 8:21, 23 NLT)

"If the world is ever again to get on its feet,
the church will have to get on its knees."

UNKNOWN

90. The Volleyball Player

Amanda called from college in tears last week. "Jeannie, would you pray for me?"

"Trouble with the coach again?" I asked. My young prayer daughter attends a division one university on a volleyball scholarship. As one of the youngest members on the team, she struggles to keep up.

"It was the worst ever." She paused for a moment. "The coach stopped the scrimmage to yell at me in front of everyone. She shrieked, 'Amanda! Work. Work! *Work!*' She made the whole team stop and hold their balls quiet. And she kept screaming and screaming at me. She was so mad she kicked the bleachers. Then she yelled that everyone should leave—just leave! She couldn't hold practice if Amanda was going to ruin everything by not trying." Amanda's voice broke.

"I'm so sorry, sweetheart."

"You know the funny thing." Amanda sniffed. "I thought I was trying my hardest." We talked a few minutes more, then prayed over the phone for God to comfort her and help her shine for him through her trials. We asked him to help her maintain a sweet attitude, to keep the drills straight in her mind, to give her confidence. We prayed for the coach who had taken out her own frustrations on a young university student.

Two days later I prayed over the e-mail for Amanda, asking God to give her some small affirmation from the coach. As soon as I typed the prayer, I changed my mind. The coach had treated her with disdain all year, she would never say anything nice to Amanda. I backtracked and deleted my request, but felt a check in my spirit. *Tell me what to pray, Lord.* I said.

Moments later, my fingers flew over the keyboard quoting Psalm 5:12, then asking the Lord to bless Amanda. *Lord, surround her with your love and favor. Allow her to feel your presence. And let the coach express appreciation for her in some small way today.* I smiled ruefully and shook my head. Not only was I asking God for the impossible, I was demanding it *today*. I wondered if I had faith for that.

The following morning Amanda wrote back. "God answered your prayer for that word of assurance yesterday. The coach went through the team and told each person whether they were doing good or not. Many girls got a no. Some got good. She told me I was doing pretty good. I will take that. Thanks for the prayers. Love, Amanda."

(JST)

"For surely, O LORD, you bless the righteous; you surround them with your favor as with a shield." (Ps. 5:12)

91. Old Roots, New Fruits

Joan hurried down the nursing home corridor, trying not to breathe in the unpleasant odors oozing from each doorway. She couldn't believe her father-in-law had to live in a place like this. But since he broke his hip a year ago, he required complete care, more than the family could handle. They'd moved him from one care facility to another, searching for a pleasant home for him. They hadn't found it yet.

She pasted a happy look on her face, poked her head into room 107, calling out in her most cheerful voice, "Knock. Knock."

Harold greeted her by wiggling his ears, his signature gesture. They chatted for a while, each of them trying to stay upbeat, but it didn't work. Harold felt useless.

"This is worse than prison," he said.

Joan patted his hand. "I know." He had spent his entire life doing for other people. Giving unselfishly. Now here he lay, bedridden. He couldn't even transfer from the bed to his wheelchair without help.

Half an hour after she arrived, Joan left. As she walked back down the hallway, she prayed the same prayer she prayed every day. *Lord, give Harold a home that doesn't stink. And help him feel useful again.* She didn't believe

God could answer. They'd checked every care facility in town and found nothing suitable.

But amazingly, a few weeks later, Joan heard about a new facility for the elderly. When she and her husband drove over to check it out, she couldn't believe her eyes. Six acres of manicured grounds complete with fountains and pools of swimming koi spread across a hilltop site with a panoramic view of mountains and the river.

No residents had moved in yet. Two caregivers with their three children occupied the bottom floor of the opulent facility. Twelve brand-new apartments stood empty, waiting for elderly residents.

And they wanted Harold.

A short time later, Joan moved him into an apartment smelling of new carpet and fresh paint. At dinnertime that evening, she helped a caregiver wheel him into the spacious family kitchen. The aroma of meatloaf and gravy wafted through the room. The table sparkled with blue-willow dishes. The three young children, already seated around the table, politely waited for Harold to take his place at the head of the table, then they dug into their food.

"Ahem!" Harold cleared his throat. The children stopped eating and looked at him.

"We don't eat until we pray," Harold announced.

Three sets of eyes grew big. Obviously, they were not accustomed to saying grace before a meal. Three hands carefully set their silverware on their plates.

"Take the hand of the person next to you," Harold commanded. They tentatively joined hands to form a circle.

"Close your eyes." They did. And Harold raised his voice in a magnificent prayer.

Over the next year, the building gradually filled. But Harold never lost his place of authority at the head of the table. The children and residents expected him to pray before each meal. No one ever ate a bite before Harold started the meal.

In the evenings, the children sat on the floor in his apartment reading the Christian picture books Joan left in the room. When the children went to school, the employees who worked at the home streamed into Harold's apartment to sit and chat. He told them about the Lord at every opportunity. And at night, when he couldn't sleep, Harold prayed for their salvation.

The Lord had answered Joan's prayer to make her father-in-law useful. By setting him in the middle of his own personal mission field in a lovely new home, God enabled Harold to bear fruit in his old age.

(JST)

"They will still bear fruit in old age, they will stay fresh and green, proclaiming, 'The LORD is upright; he is my Rock, and there is no wickedness in him.'" (Ps. 92:14, 15)

92. No Bitterness

A few weeks after a neighbor led thirteen-year-old Heidi to the Lord, her father molested her for the first time. Shocked and confused, Heidi didn't know what to do. When she finally found the courage to tell her mother, her mother called her a liar—and nothing changed. Every day Heidi begged God to protect her. He comforted and sustained her, but the abuse continued until she left home at eighteen.

Even though she couldn't understand why God didn't answer her prayer, Heidi determined not to become bitter. Whenever hatred for her father came over her, she forced herself to replace it with prayer for him. Over time, God helped Heidi forgive.

Years later, she sat by his bedside as he lay dying. No hatred for him marred her spirit; no bitterness twisted her soul. She stayed with him, quieting his fears, talking about her Savior, until shortly before he breathed his last, she led him to the Lord.

At the funeral, she understood for the first time. God had answered her youthful prayer for protection by preserving the thing that mattered most—her untarnished spirit.

(JST)

"Above all else, guard your heart, for it affects everything you do." (Prov. 4:23 NLT)

93. The Eyes Have It

Teachers discovered Kirsten Norgaard's visual impairment in the fourth grade when she didn't pass her eye test, and glasses couldn't correct the problem. Doctors put a name to it in her fifth grade year—Stargardts. The prognosis: her vision would get progressively worse. She would lose central vision completely; and her peripheral vision would be poor. She would probably never go totally blind, but she would be legally blind soon.

Immediately after the diagnosis, she started praying for the Lord to heal her eyes. So far, the answer to that prayer has been no. But every subsequent prayer, he has answered yes.

As her eyesight worsened and studies seemed overwhelming, she begged God for help. He supplied the strength and ability for her to keep her 'A' average. Still, depression dragged her down. *I don't want to be a complainer,* she told God. *Please help me accept this.*

He spoke to her as she read the Scriptures, "I never give my children more than they can bear. I allowed this difficulty in your life because I know you can handle it. My strength will be revealed because of your weak eyesight." From then on, whenever discouragement settled over her, Kirsten remembered God's words and rebounded from self-pity into acceptance.

In her senior year of high school, Kirsten prayed to find the right college, and God directed her to an expensive Christian university she could not afford. "No loans," her parents said.

She responded by asking God for help and reassuring her parents. "I think they'll give me a scholarship because of my straight 'A' average and all the community service I've done."

She was right. Her freshman year cost her only five hundred dollars. One of her roommates, who had equally good grades in high school, paid thousands—even after receiving the best scholarship the school had to offer.

As Kirsten's senior year and student teaching approached, she ordered a Clarity Classmate—a small camera wired to a closed-circuit television. It would enable her to enlarge books and papers in the classroom so she could read aloud to the children and grade their work. Though she ordered it nearly a year in advance, checked on it numerous times over the months, and prayed that all would go smoothly, two weeks before she was to start student teaching it still had not come. The lady who was supposed to have sent for it months earlier told Kirsten it couldn't possibly arrive for several more weeks—too late for her first classroom assignment.

Once again, Kirsten fell to her knees. *Oh, Lord, I can't teach without a Clarity Classmate.* She asked friends to pray. Within two days, the woman called back. "It's the strangest thing. One of our sales representatives just got in the exact machine you wanted. He had planned to use it as a sample, but he'll let you have it."

Kirsten breathed a prayer of thanks to the Lord and prepared to begin her part-time student teaching. But the greatest challenge of her life lurked just around the corner. "I'm afraid your supervising teacher won't accept you into her classroom," the head of the program informed Kirsten.

The words slammed Kirsten like a punch in the solar plexus. "What?"

"She doesn't think you should ever be allowed to teach."

Kirsten couldn't understand what he meant. "But . . . why?"

"She thinks having a blind teacher would be unfair to elementary school children."

Depression swept over Kirsten. She had worked twice as hard as everyone else to complete her course work. Would one woman prevent her from achieving her goal, keep her from helping the children she loved? Heartbroken, she begged God for a solution.

It came from the principal of the elementary school. "I've told the teacher she has to let you try," he told Kirsten.

"Thank you. I'll change her mind about me," Kirsten promised.

She worked hard to please the supervising teacher, refusing even to use the Clarity Classmate when the teacher was around. If the teacher asked her to a read a picture book to the children, Kirsten memorized the words the night before. Paper grading was done at home. None of the children ever guessed Kirsten had a disability; they loved her as much as she loved them.

When the part-time teaching ended, Kirsten wrote, thanking the teacher for the opportunity and requesting a recommendation. The teacher declined. Kirsten learned later that the teacher told the principal she "hated to encourage Kirsten toward teaching" because "she can't even drive. How would she get to a job?"

Kirsten's prayers changed. *I can't do my full-time student teaching unless you help me,* she told the Lord. *Please give me a supervising teacher who will accept me. Give me a good experience.*

Once again, God answered with a "yes." Kirsten's new teacher welcomed Kirsten and her Clarity Classmate into the school. "The children will benefit from exposure to someone who deals so well with a disability," she said. And she offered glowing recommendations when Kirsten's tenure ended. "She did a beautiful job," she wrote. "She will be a fabulous teacher. Not one parent or student complained. We all loved her."

Now Kirsten is praying for a teaching job after graduation. There will be problems, she knows. How will she get to work since she can't drive? And if she lives close to school, will she be able to find a church within walking distance?

More difficulties will arise as time goes on. When she marries and has children, how will she get them to baseball practice? But she knows one thing for certain, God will not give her more than she can bear. And as long as she continues to ask for his help, she will come through it all victoriously.

(JST)

"No, in all these things we are more than conquerors through him who loved us." (Rom. 8:37)

94. Uncle Charles

My uncle Charles has lived a life of ceaseless prayer and ministry. All his life, he longed to shine as an example of Christ, reflecting his Lord to others. He prayed for that daily. He prayed to remain sweet in old age, serving the Lord without complaint.

I can prove God answered those prayers.

In his eighties now, he cares for his wife in assisted living. Though she is kind, dementia muddles her mind. Recently, she insisted he change her dress six times before they could go down to dinner. He lovingly complied.

Health problems plague him; doctors say he needs heart surgery. He has spent several days in the hospital over the last few months for different ailments. Yet, he added these words in longhand to the Christmas card he sent over the holidays. I quote:

"Jesus is indescribably wonderful! This might be the most wonderful Christmas season we have ever had. The Eternal, All Mighty, All Holy and All Loving Word became flesh and dwelt among us. What a mystery! What a miracle! And what a meaning! Praise the Lord! Praise his name forever! Pearl and I are doing pretty well in every way, considering our age and all. You, all of you, are remembered daily as I pray. Glory to God in the highest!"

(JST)

"Rejoice in the Lord always. I will say it again: Rejoice! Let your gentleness be evident to all. The Lord is near." (Phil. 4:4, 5)

95. The *Sectanti*

Veronica knew high school would be difficult. No laws in Romania prevented teachers from persecuting Christian students. So before school commenced her freshman year, she bolstered her courage through prayer. *I don't ask for a miracle, Jesus. Just help me stand for you without fear.* Then she marched into her first period biology class expecting mistreatment.

She got it.

As the pupils filed into the classroom and took their seats, the teacher paced the front of the room, his arms crossed over his chest, studying the teens with narrowed eyes. Veronica sat on a wooden two-person bench desk with another girl.

The teacher stopped and rested both palms on a desk in the front, leaning forward to rake his gaze over the students. The first words out of his mouth were, "Any *Sectanti* here?" His eyes halted on her.

Veronica suppressed a shudder. She knew he meant Christians, even though the term he used referred to unspeakably monstrous people who killed their own children and drank the blood. *Help me*, she prayed as she stood slowly and tilted her chin. "I am a Christian."

A smirk twisted the teacher's face. All eyes turned to stare at Veronica, and the inquisition began. The teacher misquoted the Bible, twisting its meaning, firing questions at the young freshman, insisting she answer. He ridiculed her every response. Biology could wait. She felt not a twinge of fear.

All through that year, the process repeated itself nearly every day, and God answered Veronica's prayers by giving her the strength to stand unafraid.

She didn't ask for a miracle; he didn't send one—at least not at that time.

The miracle arrived later. Veronica' father escaped from Romania, and the communist government permitted the rest of the family to immigrate to the United States to join him.

(JST)

"It is for freedom that Christ has set us free." (Gal. 5:1)

96. Nancy and Carolyn

Nancy had been praying for her daughter's mysterious illness for three years. She prayed daily for Carolyn's healing, often many times a day. It was at the end of the three years of praying that the doctor's finally diagnosed Carolyn's sickness. It was Nieman Picks—a terminal disease.

"You don't have enough faith," said fellow teachers at the Christian school where Nancy taught. "If you did, God would touch her."

A stranger in the grocery store stopped to place fervent hands on Carolyn's head, mashing down her blonde hair. "Have faith in Jesus name," she urged. "If you have faith, he will heal you."

For several years, Nancy suffered guilt because of their words. It must be her fault that Carolyn couldn't run and play with the other ten-year-olds. Nancy feared her weak faith kept her daughter confined to a wheelchair, taking her food through a feeding tube. If she could just believe . . .

But she did believe. Like Shadrach, Meshach, and Abednego in the Book of Daniel, she told the Lord, *I know you can heal her if you choose to.*

Eventually, she understood that it was God's decision—not hers. The misplaced accusations of friends and strangers couldn't matter to her. She needed to focus all her energies on keeping up the twenty-four-hour-a-day care her daughter needed.

And though God answered no to Carolyn's healing, he answered yes to many other prayers. When Nancy prayed for God to help her forgive people who continued to misunderstand, he replaced resentment with love. When Nancy pled with him for help just to make it through the day, he not only upheld her, but he often wrapped her with joy in the midst of unpleasant tasks. When she begged him to bless Carolyn, she could see Jesus' loveliness glow through her daughter's expressive eyes.

For sixteen years, Nancy never stopped praying for Jesus to heal her daughter. She prayed it right up until Carolyn's death.

Then, though Nancy's heart was filled with grief, it also overflowed with prayers of praise and gratitude as she remembered the most important request she had ever made—the prayer for her daughter's salvation. God had begun to answer when her daughter was little and could still talk. He prompted Carolyn to ask, *Dear Jesus, please forgive my sins, come into my heart, and take me to heaven to live with you when I die.*

When he entered her daughter's heart as a child, the first part of Nancy's prayer was answered. At the instant of Carolyn's death, Jesus transported her to her heavenly home. The prayer for her daughter's salvation was complete.

(JST)

"In my Father's house are many rooms; if it were not so, I would have told you. I am going there to prepare a place for you. And if I go and prepare a place for you, I will come back and take you to be with me that you also may be where I am." (John 14:2, 3)

97. Kidnapped

Juno e-mail printed **Friday, 30 March 2001**

Dear prayer warriors and friends,

Please pray with us. We are desperate. Our need is a matter of life and death. My cousin, Carlos, was kidnapped today as he was driven to work at the factory he owns in San Salvador, El Salvador. Carlos' chauffeured limousine was forced off the road. Several witnesses saw him being pushed into a car at gunpoint. No one got the license number. Pray he will not be killed. No ransom note has been delivered. I will keep you updated.

Love, Patricia

Juno e-mail printed **Friday, 30 March 2001**

My dear friend Patricia,

Kidnapped? I can hardly believe it. Of course, we'll pray! I've called the church prayer chain. Many will soon be interceding with you for Carlos and his family. I will ask for. prayer tomorrow night at midweek service, and our Thursday morning women's group will also pray. Keep us informed. Is Carlos a Christian?

Love, Joyce

Juno e-mail printed **Sunday, 1 April 2001**

Dear interceding friends,

Thank you for your prayers for Carlos and his family. No ransom note has arrived, although it is two days since Carlos was abducted. We don't know if he is alive. Every year, many are kidnapped in El Salvador and held for huge sums of ransom. Sometimes, even when the ransom is paid, the victim is killed. Twenty years ago, my uncle was kidnapped. Although millions of dollars were paid, we never saw Paul again. Of course, Carlos' family is terrified the same thing could happen to him. His wife and children are in a safe house guarded by police. My cousin, Ernesto, will negotiate for the family when the kidnappers phone. Carlos is not a Christian, but Ernesto is. Pray God will use him especially at this time. Thank you for your prayers.

My love, Patricia

Juno e-mail printed **Monday, 2 April 2001**

Lord God, be with Carlos and keep him safe. Help his terrified family trust you. Cause the kidnappers to make contact with the family this week. Let nothing go wrong, Lord. Give Ernesto wisdom as he negotiates with the bandits. Cause them to be satisfied with the amount of ransom offered. Please keep Carlos safe and well. Return him to his family. Use this whole situation for your glory. Amen.

Sending love, Joyce

Juno e-mail printed **Tuesday, 3 April 2001**

Dear praying friends,

The ransom note finally arrived. The kidnappers want an obscene amount of money—millions. If Marie can hear his voice on the phone, she will pay the ransom. Pray with us that the kidnappers will allow him to phone soon. Pray for Marie and the children to trust God in this ordeal. At least ten churches in Europe and the U. S. are interceding for Carlos—scores of Christians crying out to God. Thank you! Thank you!

Patricia

Juno e-mail printed **Thursday, 5 April 2001**

Dear friends,

Carlos phoned Marie today! He is alive! The ransom money has been dropped at the specified site. We know from experience that we have no guarantee. This is the most dangerous time. Pray he won't be killed.

Love to all, Pat

Juno e-mail printed **Wednesday, 18 April 2001**

Dear Patricia,

It's been two weeks since your last report. What is happening with Carlos?

Blessings, Joyce

Juno e-mail printed **Thursday, 26 April 2001**

My dear friends,

Twenty-eight days ago, Carlos was kidnapped. The family has heard nothing since ransom was paid; they are despairing for his life. But we know that with God all things are possible. We continue to covet your prayers for him. Only God can spare his life.

Yours, Patricia

Juno e-mail printed **Saturday, 28 April 2001**

Father God, Have mercy, Father. Save Carlos' life. Don't let him be killed. Bring him home to his family. Be his escape. Help him to not give up; instead, give him favor with his captors so they will set him free. We trust you are working, Lord. Thank you.

My love and prayers, Joyce

Juno e-mail printed **Tuesday, 8 May 2001**

Prayer partners,

Thirty-nine days without word of Carlos. Still we believe. God has all power, and we are trusting in his faithfulness.

Waiting, Patricia

Juno e-mail printed **Friday, 11 May 2001**

Our Thursday group bombarded heaven for Carlos again today. Because God is silent does not mean he is saying no. We continue to seek the Lord for Carlos. Trust. God is for us.

My love, Joyce

Juno e-mail printed **Friday, 18 May 2001**

Praise be to God! Carlos is home! He's been released without harm. We are ecstatic! Thank you, God! Thank you, prayer warriors!

With an overflowing heart, Patricia

Juno e-mail printed **Saturday, 19 May 2001**

Wow! Praise God! Hooray for Jesus! I will pass the word on to the Oregon intercessors. We rejoice with you! Thank you, wonderful Father.

My love, Joyce

(PP)

"For there is one God and one mediator between God and men, the man Christ Jesus, who gave himself as a ransom for all men—the testimony given in its proper time." (1 Tim. 2:5, 6)

"Prayer is not the mystical experience of a few special people, but an aggressive act . . . an act that may be performed by anyone who will accept the challenge to learn to pray."

JACK HAYFORD

98. Praying to Die

Glenn climbed onto his riding mower and shoved the key into the ignition. *Why do you ignore me, Lord? I've been praying the same prayer every day since Dorothy died—twelve years! Why won't you answer it?*

Yanking out the choke, Glenn pumped the gas, and the engine jerked to life. *I just wanted to enjoy retirement with my wife. Was that too much to ask?*

He whipped the mower out onto the grass and started the first sweep across his two-acre lot. *It isn't fair. Dorothy and I raised five good kids. I served as Sunday-school superintendent for twenty years. Then as soon as I retired, you took her. I'm tired of this life. I want to see Dorothy, and I want to see you.* The roar of the motor covered the sound of his voice. But it didn't matter. He could yell if he wanted to, and no one would hear.

Glenn lived alone—lonely.

There's nothing left for me down here. The kids have their own lives. My diabetes has left me nearly blind. He maneuvered the tractor close to the creek bank. *All I ask is that you let me die. Please let me die.*

Glenn felt the mower shift in the loose soil at the edge of the bank. He jerked the steering wheel to correct the error, but the mower pitched sideways into the creek. The next thing he knew, the heavy tractor pressed down on his chest, pinning him to the creek bed. His head was under water. He couldn't move. He couldn't breathe. He knew he was about to die.

God was answering his prayer! He'd see Dorothy and Jesus in moments!

But instead of the peace he had anticipated, horror gripped Glenn. He didn't know how he knew, but for the first time, he knew why God had refused to answer his prayer. The prayer was wrong!

He had no right to ask God to take him. In asking to die, he had usurped God's authority. And now he would have to meet God, knowing what a selfish, terrible thing he had done. He couldn't bear it.

Forgive me, God! Glenn struggled to extricate himself, but the tractor held him fast. He pushed against the weight of the tractor with his free hand. *I was wrong, God!* He couldn't hold his breath much longer. *I know I don't deserve it, but please keep me from dying!*

Suddenly, though he wasn't aware of doing anything to change the position of his head, air surrounded his face, and he sucked in gasping, choking breaths. *Thank you, Lord.*

For another twenty minutes, Glenn worked to pull free of the tractor and drag himself out of the creek. Then, for the first time in twelve years, Glenn lifted his voice in gratitude to God. *Lord, you are so merciful. For twelve years, you refused to answer my misguided prayer. But you answered immediately when I begged you to save my life. Thank you.*

(JST)

"For God is greater than our hearts, and he knows everything." (1 John 3:20)

99. Julie's Hope

Julie desperately wanted a child. Through one brief marriage and several live-in relationships, she pled with God to give her a baby, but she remained childless. Lonely. Empty.

Then, as she neared forty, Julie dedicated her life to the Lord, and a wonderful thing happened. God sent her a family—a loving Christian husband and his eleven-year-old son. And since the boy's mother had deserted him years earlier, Julie became Jordan's mom. She doted on him, lavishing all her stored-up mother's affection on her amazing new son. They giggled together in quiet after-school moments, and Julie talked with him about the Lord in the evenings. Finally, shortly after Jordan turned sixteen, he became a Christian. Julie had never been happier.

But despite Julie's love and dedication and Jordan's new relationship with the Lord, Jordan suffered from past years of pain. One August afternoon while Julie and her husband, Jaime, attended a wedding, fresh rejection in the form of a letter arrived from Jordan's biological mother. The letter mixed together with other problems, eventually pushed Jordan over the edge. When Julie and her husband returned home that afternoon and Julie opened the front door, she saw her beloved son hanging at the top of the stairs.

For a moment, horror froze her body, then a scream wrenched loose from deep inside her. Her husband pushed past her and bounded to the top of the stairs. Julie stumbled after him. Jaime threw his arms around Jordan's legs, lifting the weight of his son's six-foot-five-inch frame while Julie's numbed fingers clawed at the rope strangling Jordan's neck. The instant they freed him, Jaime eased him onto the floor, wiped the vomit from his mouth, and began performing mouth-to-mouth resuscitation. Julie, shaking violently, rushed to the phone and called 911.

Minutes later, sirens blared. Paramedics rushed up the stairs to help.

But it was too late. Jordan's waxen gray color told the unthinkable truth. One of the paramedics, his face furrowed with compassion, turned to Julie, "I'm sorry. . ." He paused. "Your boy didn't really want to die. See." He indicated obvious signs of struggle on Jordan's body. "He thrashed around trying to free himself. He wanted to live."

Rasping sobs wracked Julie. As in a dream, she watched her husband scoop Jordan's limp body into his arms and carry him down the stairs. Clutching his son, Jaime strode through the house, out the back door, and into the sunlit backyard. Dazed, Julie trailed after them, forming a private funeral procession. In the middle of the grass and flowers, Jaime held Jordan high, looked heavenward, and cried out, "He's yours now, God. I give him to you." Then Julie and Jaime grieved together, clinging to their beautiful blonde son for one last time.

The next few months were the worst of Julie's life. Though she loved her husband, she had never felt so empty. She begged God for help in her sorrow, but the only thing that comforted her through aching grief was the memory of Jordan's conversion and the knowledge that he had regretted his momentary weakness and tried to live. He was with Jesus now.

But it wasn't enough. Julie had lost her only child, the child she had prayed for. The only child she would ever have. She was forty-four years old. She had no hope that the pain in her heart could ever ease. The Bible claims that God never gives us more than we can bear, but this felt like more than Julie could bear.

Then in February, three days after what should have been Jordan's eighteenth birthday, Julie missed her monthly cycle. A subsequent pregnancy test showed positive. God had opened Julie's womb!

Over the next few months as Julie's body grew, joy gradually mingled with her pain. Tests revealed that her baby was a girl; Julie lifted her heart in praise to the Lord. Gratitude was her daily companion as she thought about the perfect name for her miracle baby.

Today, Julie dotes on her new daughter, even though she still cries for Jordan every day. He'll always be her son. Nothing can ever replace him.

But now she has Hope.

(JST)

"Sons are a heritage from the LORD, children a reward from him." (Ps. 127:3)

"The most powerful kind of prayer has nothing to do with style, polish, technique, or a particular arrangement of impressive-sounding words. It's simply a child of God crying out to heaven."

RON MEHL,

A Prayer That Moves Heaven

100. Ray's Cow

By the time Ray realized his favorite cow needed help and called the veterinarian, he was afraid it was too late to save her calf. Holly lay on bare ground under the pear tree, too weak to push any more, too weak to stand up.

"How long has she been in labor?" the doctor asked.

Ray looked at me.

"At least seven hours," I said.

The vet pulled on a rubber glove that reached all the way to his armpit, then shoved his arm into the cow's birth canal in search of the calf. Holly groaned, but she didn't try to get up. "The baby's turned the right way. That's good." The doctor pulled his arm out, picked up the end of a chain and, holding it in his right hand, plunged his right arm back in up to the armpit again. He and the cow both grunted as he strained to attach the chain to the calf's hooves.

The job done, he pulled his arm out and grasped the handle of the calf jack. "How long's she been down?" He panted as he cranked the handle. The cow stretched her head back and groaned again. Tears poured from her eyes.

"Three or four hours," Ray said.

"That's bad. You got to get her up on her feet, or she'll die." The chain clanked as the vet continued to turn the handle.

A sucking sound, and the calf slipped out and plopped onto the ground, followed by an ooze of blood. The vet sprang to release the calf's hooves from the chain. "It's alive!" he announced. "No wonder the mom couldn't get him out. He's huge."

Holly tried to turn her head to see her baby. Ray and I grabbed the slippery calf and dragged him close to Holly's head. The cow made a feeble attempt to lick him. The calf struggled to his feet and stumbled away from his mom. "You'd better get towels and rub him down," the vet said. "The mom's too weak to do it." I hurried for towels.

Ray pulled the hose over. The vet slid the rush of water over his glove and hands as he talked. "The mom may not make it. She's been down too long. I've never seen one live past twelve hours. They're so heavy they get nerve damage from lying on their side, and then they can't get up. Like when your foot goes to sleep at night. Only she weighs 1,800 pounds."

"Yeah." Ray filled a green plastic bucket and tipped it so Holly could drink. "We'll try to get her up," he promised the vet. Holly sucked in water, then dropped her head listlessly. I returned with the towels and handed one to the doctor before she started rubbing down the calf. Holly fastened her eyes on me, warily watching the human work on her baby.

"See that?" The vet gestured toward the cow as he dried himself. "Love for her baby is the only thing that can get her back on her feet."

"Maybe there's something else," I suggested. "I called a couple of friends to pray when I went for the towels." The vet didn't respond.

"We'll get her up," Ray assured him. He silently began praying for Holly to live.

The vet loaded his truck. "Twelve hours!" he said as he drove off. "If she's not up by then, she'll never make it."

For the rest of the day, we tried everything we could think of to encourage Holly onto her feet. We prayed as we hauled water and grain to her. We draped a tarp from the limbs of the pear tree to shade her when the sun moved. We lugged the calf to her udder and helped him nurse.

Though it seemed cruel, we yelled at Holly and smacked her flank, urging her up. We got behind her and shoved her huge frame back and forth repeatedly, hoping the momentum would provide the extra push Holly needed. She understood and rocked with us, her legs pawing at the ground, but she couldn't muster the strength to stand.

By evening, we'd given up. Thirteen hours had passed. Holly lay still as death. The vet was right; the situation was hopeless. We took the calf to the barn and bottle-fed it.

In the morning, Ray checked on the cow before his morning coffee. After looking her over carefully, he called the rendering company and scheduled a visit for them to pick her up.

"Wait," I called, looking through the window, "I saw her ear twitch."

Ray sighed into the phone. "I guess you'll have to finish her off," he told the rendering company.

"We don't do that," the lady in the office said. "Call us back when she's dead."

The next few hours were torture for Ray and me. Holly wouldn't even move when we tried to give her water or grain. We hated watching her suffer. We wished we could euthanize her to put her out of her misery, but we had no way to do that.

Twenty-four hours after Holly lay on the ground to deliver her calf, we left to pick up some nails at Home Depot, hoping to get our minds off the dying cow. When we drove in our driveway an hour later, Ray forced himself to glance sideways at Holly's resting place under the pear tree.

He gasped. "She's gone!"

"No way!" My head whipped around.

Ray's eyes scanned the field. Twenty feet from the pear tree, Holly stood munching on hay. "There!" He pointed. "She's up! Oh my goodness, she's up! How . . . ?"

"It had to be the prayers," I whispered. "The vet's not going to believe this."

"I can hardly believe it," Ray murmured. "And I'm looking at it."

(JST)

"He blessed them, and their numbers greatly increased, and he did not let their herds diminish." (Ps. 107:38)

101. Put Teela to Sleep

Our Australian shepherd dog sliced across the field, racing ahead of my car as I drove down our long, winding gravel drive. She knew I was headed to pick up Tevin from kindergarten, and she intended to beat me to the bus stop at the end of our road. By cutting corners and running at near cheetah speed, she always reached the corner several seconds before I did.

Today was no exception. She reached the blacktop ahead of me and pranced near the bus stop, eyeing my minivan, tail wagging. She didn't notice the red car speeding toward her. But I saw it. I drove faster, screaming her name and honking my horn.

Oblivious to the danger, Teela reacted to my warnings with joy—jumping up and down, barking excitedly. I reached the end of the driveway a split second after the car fishtailed into her. At the last minute, I averted my eyes, but I'll never forget the sickening sounds. Brakes squealed. Teela yelped in pain—and kept yelping.

The car screeched to a halt, pinning Teela's leg under the back wheel. She drew into a sit-up position against the pain. Her terrified crying rammed my senses, mingling with my screams.

I leapt from my van, running toward Teela, frantically shouting at the woman driver of the red car. "You're on her leg!" The woman looked confused, dazed.

"Move your car! It's still on her leg!"

A look of understanding flitted over the woman's face, and she backed up a few inches, releasing my dog. Teela stopped yelping and limped toward me on three legs, whimpering. Her back left leg hung limply, a bloody red sliver.

Out of the corner of my eye, I saw the yellow kindergarten bus pull up, red lights flashing. Tevin hopped out and skipped toward me.

Teela licked my hand, and I bent over her, stroking her head, breathing hard.

The woman from the red car tugged on my arm. "I'm so sorry."

"It wasn't your fault," I mumbled. Tevin walked slowly toward me now, his eyes fastened on his dog. Teela whined and nuzzled my hand.

"Get in the car, sweetie," I called to Tevin. "I'll be there in a second." He paused, then went to stand by the van. I couldn't figure out what to do next.

"I'm so sorry," the woman moaned over and over.

"No, no. She ran out in front of you," I assured her. I didn't have time to comfort her right now. My mind wouldn't work.

Tevin watched us intently. I walked toward my van with Teela following. How could she keep walking with that leg?

How could I get her home? She was a farm dog. She'd never ridden in the car. I couldn't carry her.

I slid open the van door for Tevin. Teela jumped in and lay down, bleeding all over the blue mat. The dog had more sense than I did in an emergency.

Tevin climbed in the front seat beside me. We drove slowly back up the drive, the gravel crunching beneath our tires, and stopped in front of our house. I sat with my hands on the wheel, feeling overwhelmed. Stunned. What should I do? I knew Ray would not want the huge expense of taking a dog to the vet.

Tevin rested his head on my shoulder, "Let's pray, Mommy."

"Oh, yes." Why hadn't I thought to pray earlier? Maybe I had. I couldn't remember. I bowed my head, praying aloud past the lump in my throat. Tears flowing. *Show me how to help our dog, Lord. Give me wisdom.*

Pwease help her, God, Tevin added. He kissed my cheek, and I wrapped him in a hug. Then, together, Tevin and I helped our dog into the house. We spread out a shaggy orange rug in the entry for her. She lay on it with her head on Tevin's leg, whimpering as he patted her neck.

"I'm going to call Daddy at work," I told Tevin. I took a deep breath and punched in the number. When Ray answered, I told him about the accident. "Is it okay if I take Teela to the vet?" I asked. "She has to have help."

He paused. "You know we can't afford it."

"Please." I turned my face away so Tevin wouldn't see my despair. "Can't I just take her to the vet and find out how much it will cost?" *Lord, please make him let me take her in*, I prayed. *I can't stand seeing her suffer like this.*

He sighed. "Okay. Take her in. But call me before you run up too many charges."

As soon as Tevin's older brother and sister arrived home from school, the four of us carried Teela to the car. As we drove to the vet, I prayed aloud, *Please, Lord. If there is anyway possible, save Teela's life.*

Twenty minutes later, I called Ray from the phone in the doctor's office. "The vet says she has to have surgery," I told him.

"We don't have hundreds of dollars to spend on a dog," my husband said. "Tell the vet to put her to sleep."

My body heaving with sobs, I signed the papers so the vet could euthanize our beloved dog. "I'm sure the doctor will do it right away so she won't have to suffer," the girl behind the counter told me. I nodded, crying too hard to thank her. Grief-stricken, the kids and I drove home, everyone sobbing aloud.

Except Tevin. He seemed unconcerned.

I knew I had to help him face the truth. "Tevin, the doctor is putting Teela to sleep, and we won't see her again. Not ever."

Tevin smiled. *Teewa's not going to die.*

"Yes. She is going to die." I said it firmly. "I signed the papers and paid the doctor to do it. She is probably dead already." At that thought, fresh grief flooded over me.

Tevin's older brother and sister tried to help me explain it to him. But he refused to understand. He just shook his head, smilingly unconvinced. "No, she won't die. I pwayed for God to save her."

In my grief, I felt almost angry with his naivete. But I didn't have the energy to deal with it right then. I knew I would have to, however. Even children have to learn to face death.

The next day, Saturday, sadness turned to depression, and I wanted to nap all day. Instead, I helped my husband nail baseboard in the studio he was building for me. Over in the corner, two oil-portrait commissions stood half-finished. I didn't feel like working. Occasionally, my two oldest children wandered in to cling to me and cry. Tevin simply asked when Teela was coming home.

On Sunday, church didn't make me feel any better. And when Tevin suggested it was time to pick up Teela from the vet, I grabbed him in frustration. Holding onto his shoulders, I looked directly into his eyes and spoke firmly, almost harshly. "Tevin. Teela is dead. She's never coming home." Tevin skipped out to the sandbox, unconcerned.

Monday, Ray took the morning off work so he could stain the wood ceiling around the skylights in my studio. I varnished the cabinets. He was up on a ladder when the phone rang, so I answered.

"May I speak with Mrs. Taylor?" the voice on the phone asked.

"This is she."

"I am so embarrassed." The voice paused, then started again. "This is Kent Smith—Dr. Smith . . . your veterinarian. Uh, I don't know how to say this. I should have called sooner."

I waited, wondering what he could mean.

"I just couldn't put your dog to sleep. She is such a great dog."

I nearly shouted into the phone. "Teela is still alive?" Ray held his staining rag motionless, watching me.

"Yes. But she is sedated. I want your permission to operate on her."

My eyes locked with Ray's as I spoke to the vet, "How much would it cost?" Ray pressed his lips together and shook his head. I covered the mouthpiece and whispered. "Please, honey. I could pay for it with the money from the portrait commissions."

"Is money a problem?" the vet asked.

I hadn't meant for him to hear.

"Because if it is, I'll donate my services and just charge you for the supplies. It will only cost about seventy-five dollars."

I repeated the dollar amount for Ray. "Seventy-five dollars?" Tears streamed down my face, and I pressed my hand over the receiver again so the doctor couldn't hear my sobs. My eyes pled with Ray. I knew he wasn't hard-hearted.

Finally, he sighed and nodded. "Go ahead."

"Yes, go ahead and do the surgery!" I told the vet. "Thank you! Thank you!"

I hung up and ran to find the children. The two older children celebrated with hugs and shouts, but the news didn't surprise Tevin. Not one bit. There's nothing like the faith of a child.

(JST)

"I tell you the truth, anyone who will not receive the kingdom of God like a little child will never enter it." (Luke 18:17)

Suggested Reading

Bounds, E. M., *Power Through Prayer*, Grand Rapids: Zondervan (no date in book)

Dawson, Joy, *Intercession: Thrilling and Fulfilling*, Seattle: YWAM Publishing, 1997

Eastman, Dick, and Jack Hayford, *Living and Praying in Jesus' Name*, Carol Stream, Ill.: Tyndale House, 1998

Foster, Richard, *Prayer: Finding the Heart's True Home*, San Francisco: Harper San Francisco, 1992

Grubb, Norman P., *Rees Howells: Intercessor*, Philadelphia: Christian Literature Crusade, 1952, 1953

Guyon, Madame, *Experiencing the Depths of Jesus Christ*, Auburn, Maine: Christian Books, (no date in book)

Hayford, Jack W., *Prayer is Invading the Impossible*, New York: Ballantine, 1977

Mehl, Ron, *A Prayer That Moves Heaven*, Sister, Ore.: Multnomah, 2002

Myers, Ruth, Pamela Reeve, and Warren Myers, *31 Days of Prayers.* Sisters. Ore.: Multnomah, 1994

Sheets, Dutch, *Intercessory Prayer*, Ventura, Calif.: Regal, 1996

Taylor, Jeannie St. John, *How to be a Praying Mom*, Peabody, Mass.: Hendrickson, 2001

Taylor, Jeannie St. John, *Prayers for Troubled Times*, Chattanooga, Tenn.: AMG Publishers, 2002

Unknown Christian, An, *The Kneeling Christian*, Grand Rapids: Zondervan, 1945

I'd Love to Hear From You

Please share your answers to prayer with me (and Petey).

E-mail Jeannie at: prayingjeannie@juno.com

Check out Jeannie's website: www.artwrite.org

Or write to Jeannie at:

Jeannie St. John Taylor
PO Box 1973018
Portland, OR 97280-0730